studies in jazz

Institute of Jazz Studies
Rutgers—The State University of New Jersey
General Editors: Dan Morgenstern and Edward Berger

Mission Impossible

My *Life* in *Music*

Lalo Schifrin

Edited by
Richard Palmer

Studies in Jazz, No. 56

THE SCARECROW PRESS, INC.
Lanham, Maryland • Toronto • Plymouth, UK
2008

SCARECROW PRESS, INC.

Published in the United States of America
by Scarecrow Press, Inc.
A wholly owned subsidary of
The Rowman & Littlefield Publishing Group, Inc.
4501 Forbes Boulevard, Suite 200, Lanham, Maryland 20706
www.scarecrowpress.com

Estover Road
Plymouth PL6 7PY
United Kingdom

British Library Cataloguing in Publication Information Available

Library of Congress Cataloging-in-Publication Data

Schifrin, Lalo.
  Mission impossible : my life in music / Lalo Schifrin ; edited by Richard
Palmer.
     p. cm. — (Studies in jazz ; no. 56)
  Includes bibliographical references (p.   ), discography (p.   ), and index.
  ISBN-13: 978-0-8108-5946-3 (hardback : alk. paper)
  ISBN-10: 0-8108-5946-7 (hardback : alk. paper)
  1. Schifrin, Lalo. 2. Composers—Biography. 3. Jazz musicians—Biography.
I. Palmer, Richard, 1947– II. Title.

ML410.S2575A3 2008
780.92—dc22
[B]
                                    2008000653

⊗™ The paper used in this publication meets the minimum requirements of
American National Standard for Information Sciences—Permanence of Paper
for Printed Library Materials, ANSI/NISO Z39.48-1992.
Manufactured in the United States of Amreica.

Contents

~

CD Track Listing

I.   Mission: Impossible   3:11
      Firebird, track 4
      Aleph Records
          Publisher: Bruin Music Company

II.   Sketches of Miles   12:27
      More Jazz Meets the Symphony, track 1
      Aleph Records
      a. All Blues (Miles Davis/Arr. Lalo Schifrin)
          Publisher: Warner-Tamerlane
      b. Aranjuez (based on the 2nd Movement of Concerto of Aranjuez)
          (Joaquin Rodrigo/Arr. Lalo Schifrin)
          Publisher: Ed. Joaquin Rodrigo
      c. Four (Miles Davis/Arr. Lalo Schifrin)
          Publisher: Prestige Music
      d. So What (Miles Davis/Arr. Lalo Schifrin)
          Publisher: Warner-Tamerlane
      e. Green Dolphin Street (Bronislaw Kaper/Arr. Lalo Schifrin)
          Publisher: EMI/Robbins
      f. Move (Denzil Best/Arr. Lalo Schifrin)
          Publisher: Beechwood Music
      g. Miles (from Milestones)
          (Miles Davis/Arr. Lalo Schifrin)

e. Parker's Mood (Charlie Parker)
    Publisher: Atlantic Music Corporation
f. Donna Lee (Charlie Parker)
    Publisher: Atlantic Music Corporation
g. Now's the Time (Charlie Parker)
    Publisher: Atlantic Music Corporation
h. Lover Man (Roger Ramirez/Jimmy Davis/Jimmy Sherman)
    Publisher: MCA Music Publishing
i. Fallen Feathers (Quincy Jones)
    Publisher: Silhouette Music
j. I'll Remember April (DePaul/Johnston/Raye)
    Publisher: MCA Music Publishing
k. Repetition (Neil Jefti)
    Publisher: Warner Bros.
l. How High the Moon (Nancy Hamilton)
    Publisher: Hal Leonard Music Publishing

IX.   Tocata   14:35
      Gillespiana, track 5
      Aleph Records
          Publisher: MJQ Music

Total: 71:41

~

Foreword

Studies in Jazz is proud to add this work by the multitalented Lalo Schifrin to our list of titles. Schifrin's distinguished career is almost unmatched in both its diversity and accomplishment, and his fascinating memoirs comprise a wealth of musical and personal experiences spanning several eras and continents. Schifrin eloquently recounts his development as a musician against the backdrop of political turmoil and repression in his native Argentina. He discusses his enrollment at the Paris Conservatory, where he studied composition while working nights as a jazz pianist in the lively Paris 1950s club scene. He traces the evolution of his many major commissions in a variety of genres from both a musical and personal viewpoint, and he provides an insider's look at the musical and commercial aspects of film music and the Hollywood studios. Schifrin was interested in all types of music and incorporated South American, Arab, Cuban, Hawaiian, and many other cultures into his works before the term "world music" came into vogue. His travels to various parts of the world and his immersion into these different musical cultures are a fascinating *leitmotif*, as are his endeavors bridging the jazz and classical worlds.

Of particular interest to readers of this series, of course, is Schifrin's description of his introduction to jazz through the recordings of Beiderbecke and Armstrong, Fats Waller, Albert Ammons, and Pete Johnson; his emulation of the boogie-woogie stylists; his description of the Paris jazz scene of the 1950s; and his subsequent encounters with many of jazz's important creators, including Duke Ellington, Oscar Peterson, Sarah Vaughan, Stan Getz, Quincy

Jones, and Miles Davis. Schifrin calls his close association with Dizzy Gillespie "one of the happiest periods of my life in terms of music," and he presents a warm portrait of the great trumpeter with whom he toured in the early 1960s and for whom he composed such major works as *Gillespiana*. Finally, Schifrin discusses the genesis and evolution of his critically acclaimed *Jazz Meets the Symphony*, which he terms "a culmination, weaving together many different strands in my musical life and thought."

Like its author, this work transcends the confines of jazz or any other category. Rather, Schifrin offers frank and entertaining insights into the life of a highly cultured man, as well as a window on the many significant events and personalities he encountered during his odyssey.

Edward Berger
Series Editor

~

Acknowledgments

Lalo Schifrin would like to thank Richard Palmer, Ed Berger, Dan Morgenstern, and Renée Camus, who were very helpful on the logistic and artistic aspects of the book. Special thanks to my wife, Donna, who has always been my inspiration.

Richard Palmer likewise thanks Ed Berger, Dan Morgenstern, and Renée Camus; he also pays tribute to the helpful guidance of Michael Tucker and Ann Palmer.

PART I

ROOTS AND BEGINNINGS

~

Prologue

On the 4th of June, 1943, the Argentine army overthrew the Constitutional government of President Castillo. A group of officers sympathetic to the Axis powers hijacked the institutions, closed the Congress, and occupied the Pink House of Buenos Aires. Behind them was a colonel, Juan Domingo Peron, who was the mastermind of the plot. These officers had nationalistic ideas, and Peron was helped by the German Embassy and German financiers. He had been active for some time in the military attaché office of the Argentine Embassy in Rome, so he learned from Mussolini the art of seducing the masses. [Before that he had been expelled from Chile as an agent of the Axis powers.]

Within a short time, through intrigue and maneuvers, he became vice president and Minister of Labor in the new Argentine government. His contacts with the Nazi hierarchy were at the highest levels. One of the plans of the GOU (Group of United Officers) was to build a concentration camp in Ezeiza, near the capital. Ezeiza is today the site of the International Airport of Argentine. I was eleven years old, and perhaps the only reason I am alive today is that the allies won World War II.

Of course, Peron was also a very clever opportunist, and Stalingrad and El Alamein forced him to make Argentina a neutral country. His government finally declared war against Germany and Japan a few days before Hitler committed suicide. Obviously Peron's intentions were to make it possible for Argentina to join the United Nations.

In 1946, in order to appease international public opinion, the military government called for general elections. Peron, who was a candidate for his own party, knew how to move the propaganda machine through the press, radio, and television. Also, he organized gigantic public demonstrations. Many workers and employees were forced to go since the unions were controlled by the Peronist Party. The leader, who learned a lot from Mussolini, had charisma and was an excellent communicator. Eve Duarte de Peron, his wife, helped him (bad cop, good cop) in the seduction of the masses.

The opposition made several mistakes. The most important was to make an alliance with the Communist party, which everybody knew was an instrument of Stalin's Soviet Union. Besides, the American Embassy published a white book in which the association of Peron and the Nazis was documented in detail. The war criminals from Europe were granted asylum by the regime through Argentine consulates in Lisbon, Madrid, and Vatican sources. The intervention of the American ambassador alienated a great part of the population. The Peronist Party won the presidency as well as the Congress, the Provinces' governorships, and Legislature by 51% to 49%. Immediately an authoritarian system of government was implemented, with control of the Congress and the press plus the armed forces and the police. Argentina became, in practice, a totalitarian state. My father advised me not to talk about politics in public places and to avoid any activity that might compromise me. Anyway, I didn't belong to any political party. Like Groucho Marx, "I never wanted to belong to a club that would accept me as a member." The telephones were tapped, and there were spies all over. So I resigned myself to read and listen to the official propaganda but to find a refuge in my academic studies and music.

Some years ago, in New York City, I was working with Tim Rice on a song for a movie, and I told him this story. His reply was that "Lloyd Webber and I did a lot of research when we wrote *Evita*." Such research must have been superficial, to put it politely: that show demonstrated an ignorance of almost all the historical facts.

CHAPTER TWO

Prelude

I was born on June 21, 1932, in Buenos Aires, Argentina. My parents' address at the time was 621 Uruguay Street, very near the Teatro Colon, where my father was working. Our apartment was located on the ground floor and had a very large patio that could accommodate the full Buenos Aires Philharmonic. Its one hundred members played "Happy Birthday" for me on my fifth birthday. This gives you an idea of how popular I was amongst them. I became the orchestra's "mascot," and they all gave me gifts constantly; for example, the first bassoonist bought me the first film projector ever available in the market. The patio was so large that I was able to stage operas in which big dolls and all kinds of artifacts helped.

My parents both came from musical families. My father, Luis, was, at that time, the concertmaster (leading violin) of the Buenos Aires Philharmonic. In addition to five sisters he had two brothers, one of whom was first cello of the same orchestra; the other was a professional violinist. My aunts played everything from woodwinds to stringed instruments, as well. I was told that they were better than their brothers, but in those days professional musical activity by women was considered taboo in that patriarchal society. Nevertheless, they played chamber music in their homes, which I listened to during my frequent visits.

My mother, Clara Ester, had one sister and two brothers. My uncles were musicians, as well. My father met my mother in her parents' home when he was giving violin lessons to my uncle Sam. Obviously, I was exposed to the musical arts at an early age. I had the opportunity to attend rehearsals, recitals, ballets, and opera performances. One of the first operas I saw filled me with terror: *Lucia di Lammermoor* by Donizetti. The mad scene, in which she appeared on stage disheveled and holding a big knife, was the cause of the insomnia that to this day follows me wherever I go. I also attended rehearsals held by Arturo Toscanini (the bass drum beats made by hard mallets immediately caught my attention).

But my own musical experiences were quite disagreeable. My first piano teacher, Enrique Barenboim, whose son Daniel became a renowned pianist and conductor, was ruthless in his cruel use of a sharp pencil against my fingers every time I made a mistake. My father did not protest, and there was very little that my mother could do to protect me. This was the way that music education was practiced in those days; no Freudian approach or seduction into the spiritual world of the great masters. Only sheer repetition and the quick hits of the pencil against the knuckles, which were supposed to create a reflexive condition.[1] Obviously, I found it terrifying and boring at the same time. Nevertheless, on my own I read music by J.S. Bach, Clementi, Scarlatti, and Mozart. I cherished those solitary moments when I could really appreciate the beauty of the melodic lines in conjunction with the harmonic accompaniments.

Now that I had learned the basics about music notation, I proceeded to write down the melodies that came to my mind. The right hand was assigned with its fixation on the stave, and the accompaniment was given to the left hand in the bass clef. After contemplating the results, I realized that I was embarking on a journey, and the music paper was the symbol of a world that had to be explored and colonized. Since music also happens in time, it is possible now to arrive at the conclusion that the secret of my life is contained in those hieroglyphics that kept gradually getting more and more complex.

All this was happening when I was about six, which was when my sister Flora was born, bringing to an end my time as an only child overprotected by both parents.[2] My father oversaw the general lines of my education, but my mother took me to piano and art lessons. It felt good to be loved, and having a big family with many aunts, uncles, and cousins gave me a secure feeling of belonging. My mother's younger brother, Uncle Mauricio, was like an older brother to me, and he taught me how to play football (soccer.) He also took me to matches on Sunday afternoons. Sunday was the day in which everybody gathered at my grandmother's house. She was a sweet lady and loved me so much that I was the only one in the family that she took to Saturday afternoon movies. My preference was for westerns, thrillers, and horror films. When I was five years old, I told my classmates in grammar school that "Over the weekend I saw a horror movie, but I bet you that without the music it wouldn't have been so scary!" So we may say that another one of the branches of my future musical activities had been added. Of course, later on my taste became more refined (*Alexander Nevsky*, *Stagecoach*, *The Maltese Falcon*, and movies by De Sica, Clouzot, and Ingmar Bergman).

One Sunday afternoon, after attending a soccer match with my uncle, I asked him to go to a place where I could have some pizza and an ice cream. He said, "Your grandma is waiting for us with a succulent dinner, and she will be very hurt if you don't eat her food." I promised I wouldn't tell anyone about our secret, so we ate the pizza and my grandmother's meal as well.

We spent the summers in South Atlantic resorts. Nevertheless, a music teacher was hired to come in after lunch in order for me to keep my memory and fingers limber. Once, in Puerta del Este, Uruguay, the British Navy sunk the German battleship *Graf Spee*. The noise was tremendous, and it was a very traumatic experience. I thought about the real war in Europe, and I felt lucky that for the time being we were so far from that tragic conflict.

Back in Buenos Aires, I would play soccer and rugby in a park near my house. Once, my father witnessed these actions and became very angry with me. "What about the piano . . . your hands, your fingers!" He screamed at me and humiliated me in front of my friends. For a month I became a recluse, but during that time alone at home, I listened to my first jazz records: Bix Beiderbecke, Louis Armstrong, Fats Waller, Albert Ammons, Pete Johnson. I tried and succeeded in playing "boogie woogies" like Meade Lux Lewis.

The film *Rhapsody in Blue* was another turning point in my development. When I was nine years old, I bought the scores to Gershwin's *Concerto in F* and *Rhapsody in Blue* and I learned them. I played them for my father, and he was impressed. He took me to the Teatro Colon, where the Philharmonic music director, Erich Kleiber, gave me the opportunity to audition. Since at the time no classical music pianist in Argentina had learned Gershwin's works, Kleiber decided to let me play *Rhapsody in Blue* on a Sunday morning concert.[3]

However, there was tension in my house. My father was getting nervous and was under tremendous stress. He developed ulcers, which, in those days, had no known cure. He had terrible pains. I overheard, one day at lunch, the source of his problem, which he told my mother. One of his colleagues, a fellow violinist who sat next to him in the first chair, was sympathetic to Hitler's ideology. On his return from a trip to Germany, his violin case had accidentally opened backstage and a lot of flyers and brochures filled with Nazi propaganda spilled out.

Most of the orchestra witnessed this incident, and many musicians were subpoenaed by the House of Representatives' committee on Anti-Argentinean activities. My father was one of them; he was torn between his duties as a citizen (and his own convictions) and his loyalty to his friend. Suddenly, he was "saved by the bell." The date he was supposed to appear before the committee was in the first week of July 1943. On June 4, the Perons' coup d'état took place. The army closed the Congress and assumed power, so the testimony never took place. However, his ulcers continued to cause him suffering until the end of his life in 1978.

In 1944, I was accepted, after a very rigorous test, by the Colegio Nacional de Buenos Aires, the only secondary school institution that belonged to the University of Buenos Aires. It was very demanding and severe, but the advantage was that the graduated students could continue the advanced studies of their choice—medicine, law, economics, engineering, philosophy, so forth—without further exams. I felt I could not continue my piano studies because of the tremendous pressure of the college, which had professors from the university and did not consider us high school students.

In May 1945, most of the institution's population went onto the streets to celebrate Germany's defeat. We were chased by the Peronist mounted police. The same thing happened a few months later, when Japan surrendered. We went to Place France to sing "The Marseillaise" and the Argentine national anthem, which mentions the word *freedom* several times. This time the police used guns, and several students were killed or wounded. I spent a whole evening hidden in the branches of a high tree. The distress of my family the next day, when I returned home, was indescribable. My parents made me swear I would never get involved in any political demonstrations again.

And I could see their point, not least because politics were already contaminating the Argentinean music scene. Peron collaborators tried to interpret and apply his philosophy in every aspect of day-to-day life. Since he was a nationalist, the regime came with absurd and naïve regulations in order to "protect the Argentinean culture from Anglo-Saxon infiltration." In the movie theaters, "live" acts of tango and folk music had to be hired by the exhibitors for about a half hour before the beginning of the movie in order to display their talents. But, the theater owners, in order to save money, were bringing mediocre acts, sometimes really bad. The audiences were going to the hall to smoke a cigarette while second-rate musicians, singers, and dancers were sadly trying desperately to avoid the exodus.

This cultural protection extended to all forms of artistic events and also the recording industry. The Argentinean labels were forbidden to import records from the United States. Nevertheless, some foreign records were sold in special stores, and after my discovery of jazz, I slowly started my collection. Our weekends there were listening sessions in the houses of friends, one of whom had been able to acquire the latest novelties, such as *Charlie Parker with Strings*.

Those college days are still very vivid to me. I made new friends who were very influential in my cultural development. The level of education was such that it contributed to the expansion of my spiritual horizons.[4] But although formal studies occupied my time, including weekends, the discovery of Bud Powell, George Shearing, Thelonious Monk, Dizzy Gillespie, and Charlie Parker drew me back to the piano, and it was the technical complexity of their modern jazz that did it. Of course, I became popular at co-ed parties, but for me this was a serious matter. In Argentina we could not buy imported records due to the protectionist laws. I met a skipper with the U.S. Merchant Marine who traveled between New Orleans and Buenos Aires. He brought me catalogs of record companies with the latest jazz recordings. I ordered and paid in advance for my preferences, and forty-eight days later the records were in Buenos Aires' port. The problem was that I had to go and get them. Even in the summer, I wore a raincoat and hid the LPs around my waist, under my pants' belt.

Also, I met a group of amateur Argentinean musicians (one was a trombonist from the college), and we did jam sessions in our houses. Although my mother enjoyed my new hobby, my father was against it. Because of the improvisational style, he used to say, "If you cannot write it or read it, it is not music." However, it was for me, and I have found a parallel between jazz and some of the twentieth-century composers: Debussy, Ravel, Bartok, and Stravinsky.

After I graduated from the CNBA, I went to law school in order to appease my father. If I was not going to become a classical musician, I had to have a "serious" profession. However, at the same time, I found a great piano teacher, one of the first refugees from the Soviet Union. Andreas Karalis was his name, and he had been the director of the Kiev Conservatory. Under his tutelage, I learned the Russian school of piano technique, which is so comprehensive in its triple focus on dexterity, endurance, and control.

Around that time, I attended a lecture by an avant-garde composer, Juan Carlos Paz, who had been a disciple of Arnold Schoenberg in Vienna before the Second World War. I was so impressed and attracted to his intriguing thoughts that after one of his conferences, I asked him if he gave private lessons in composition. He took me as a disciple. His methods were very stimulating. He started with eighteenth-century harmony, analyzing Haydn, Mozart, and orchestrations by those composers. He continued with Beethoven and the romantics and ended in Wagner. Then he jumped in time to the beginning of the Middle Ages' counterpoint and worked up through the elaborate fugues of Bach. Then another jump in history, this time to the future: twentieth-century music. He gave me lessons in a café, away from the piano. Usually after lunch and around 5:00 p.m. other composers, poets, writers, and painters dropped by, and we would end up having dinner together.

By now I had reached the conclusion that music was my vocation and that I wished to drop out of law school. I told my father my decision, and he almost had a heart attack. My mother called his doctor, who told me not to break dramatic news to his patient all at once; perhaps I could do it gradually. The position of my father at this time was not so much against jazz as a valid music. He started to accept it, but he was afraid about my financial security, status, and, above all, the atmosphere attached to nightclubs where jazz was played: drugs, alcohol, and prostitutes. Now that I am a father myself, I understand his opposition. My mother shared his views but was more understanding. What they could not comprehend was that for me music was an obsession, and since they had provided me with strong moral values, there was no danger that I would fall into Faustian temptations.[5] Besides, I always kept a healthy attitude to life in general, and my inner strength was a great protection against these temptations. Nevertheless, the preoccupation of my parents was contagious, and I didn't quite know what to do or where to go, especially after a scary incident that must, I think, have happened in 1948.

On one late Saturday afternoon I was returning to my house (around 1948) carrying a special case for LPs. All of a sudden, I was detained by two individuals in civilian clothes. "Police!" they screamed. They looked quite sinister and demanded for me to open the case. When they discovered the records with English labels and the word *Jazz* on many of them, they wanted to take me to the police station. "One second," I said. "There is a café across the street and it has a piano, and I would like to play something for you." They were intrigued and followed me to the café. I opened the piano and proceeded to play a tango. They smiled and let me go. Thanks to that tango, I did not have to sleep in jail that night. Even so, the episode gave me nightmare intimations of an unhappy future—and it was then that I had another important stroke of luck.

A famous classical pianist from Austria, Friedrich Gulda, came to Buenos Aires to play concerts and recitals at the Teatro Colon. He was an extraordinary musician, only two years older than I. The rumor went around that he also played jazz. After his first recital, in which he played Galuppi, Bach, Mozart, and Ravel, a jam session was organized around him at a private home. The Argentinean musicians were professionals and only a few of them knew me. Finally, somebody told him I played piano and he invited me to sit next to him. We played four hands: he chose the bass lines, and I had the up-

per part of the piano for myself. And we started. It seems that I was doing all
the right things, coming up with good ideas, and my technique (thanks to
Karalis) was helping me to convey them with clarity and virtuosity. All of a
sudden, he looked at me, for only a moment. But that look, his intense grey-
blue eyes, gave me his tacit admiration, and it was the turning point I
needed. I felt that I had been knighted, and all my fears and doubts suddenly
seemed absurd.

Gulda and I hung out in Buenos Aires during his stay. On one occasion,
we arrived at the theater ten minutes before the recital. I knew that he had
not warmed up during the preceding hours. His manager was backstage and
was very nervous. "Do you know how you are supposed to start the concert?"
he asked. Gulda did not remember. The manager said, "The preludes and
fugues from Bach's *Whole-Tempered Harpsichord*, numbers 7, 8, 12,15 and 22."
So Gulda went to the stage and played them impeccably from memory!

We became friends. He told me that since he was born in Vienna, Mozart
was for him like folk music. It was easy for him to get in the spirit of the great
composer. I had very few opportunities to meet what I called "amphibians"—
those who feel at ease in both worlds, classical and jazz (later on I met Andre Previn, Gunther Schuller, and Dave Amram).[6] Later we kept meeting in
Los Angeles. I premiered a composition in a concert conducted by Stan Ken-
ton. On the same evening, Gulda performed his Concerto for Piano and Jazz
Band. We ended the evening at my house, playing, drinking wine and talking about how silly it was to differentiate between jazz and classical music. It
is all good music. The last time we got together was in New York City, when
I worked for my farewell concert to Dizzy Gillespie at Lincoln Center. Gulda
came to all the rehearsals and attended the concert. At the time he was playing recitals at Carnegie Hall and gigs at Birdland.

During one of Gulda's 50s visits Eva Peron died, so all concerts, movies,
and any events were canceled. With nothing to do, Gulda and I, along with
a group of his admirers, went to a friend's apartment. The silent crowds on
the street were moving slowly to pay their last respects to Evita. In the apartment, there was a concert piano and we started to play. Somebody said it
would be dangerous for us if anyone reported our musical activities. So Gulda
sat at the piano and played a Bud Powell tune with a perfect pianissimo. One
could not hear him from more than two meters away from the instrument.
This required perfect control. I've tried to practice this technique, but I could
never achieve his perfection.

Around the same time, I met one of my favorite writers, whose poetry, essays, and short stories are timeless: Jorge Luis Borges. He was losing his eye-
sight, so I often helped him to cross the street since he was giving lectures

near my house. I enrolled with some friends in the College of Superior Studies where he was teaching. I attended his classes and on many occasions I wanted to talk to him. I was eager to ask questions but I didn't dare do so. Anyway, he was so unpredictable, his thoughts coming from unusual angles and his postulates so provocative, that it was better to listen to what he had to say. On a personal level, he was extremely humble and did not want to talk about himself.[7]

One day, I had a composition class with Juan Carlos Paz. Coincidentally, he had just come back from lunch with Borges. He informed me that the Paris National Music Conservatory was granting scholarships through the French Embassy. Of course, the candidates had to go through a rigorous test, which was sent from France in a sealed envelope. He suggested that I apply. I asked him, "Do you think I have a chance?" "You have nothing to lose!" was his reply.

To my amazement, I was accepted. I needed to be in Paris by October 1952. But I could not get out of the army until February 1953, which doubled both my frustration and my dislike of the military life. I was already asphyxiated by its repressive environment, and on top of that I had seen, while serving as an assistant to a military band's captain, Argentine soldiers goose-stepping in German uniforms. However, I was rescued by a strange quirk in Argentinean military procedure.

Built into this predominantly tyrannical regime was an extraordinary sop: a few lucky soldiers could be discharged after serving six months if they won a special lottery. However, since I was a captain's assistant I was (for some never-explained reason) not allowed to participate in the lottery. In desperation I sought the help of an influential general whom I had invited to attend an opera performance at the Teatro Colon. My father gave me the tickets. General Huergo said to me, "Yes, I can get you to be part of the lottery, but I have no power to get you out of the army, you understand?" "My General, I'll appreciate any help you can offer me" was my response.

The day of the lottery, I was around a commander's huge desk in the company of nineteen soldiers. There were twenty paper balls on the desk. Two lucky guys out of twenty would win the right to be discharged immediately. The commander ordered the first soldier standing on his right to take a paper ball. He said sharply, "Do not open it yet!" While I was waiting for my turn, I saw a paper ball that was illuminated with an intense brightness by a beam of light that shone through the office window. This was not my imagination. From my angle, the vivid intensity of the ball was absolutely real. I was mesmerized by it, and my fear was that any of the other soldiers would pick it before me, since I was on the other side of the desk. But when my time came up the bright object was still there, and I took it. My heart was beating *fortissimo*. "Do not open it yet!" Finally the commander allowed us to unroll the paper balls one by one. Eighteen were empty, but mine . . . had the word *Yes* inscribed. That was it: I was free, I could go to France, and I could not believe it!

After returning my uniform and equipment I was officially discharged, although a sergeant in charge of the maintenance insulted me because of my Jewish last name. I kept my cool. The important thing was to be out, and a few hours later I was free. In Argentina, one must apply for a passport at the police department, which I did. A few weeks later I received by mail an order from the Special Section of Anti-Argentine Activities. This is an institution in which sadistic barbarians practiced torture, especially with the electric rod, while they played tangos very loudly in order to cover the victims' cries of agony. Luckily I got the mail before my parents did, otherwise they would have both had seizures. Immediately I called a lawyer friend of mine who had connections with the government. I met with him and said, "Look: now I do not want to go to Paris, and I will cancel my passport application. I do not want to be interviewed by the Special Section!" He said that once my attendance had been required I had to be there on time. "I'll tell you what. I'll be waiting in a café-bar around the corner. If you do not show up in two hours, I'll make a phone call to someone who can help you," he said. "Two hours! By that time I'll be dead, and besides, I hate physical pain!" was my agonized response.

I had to go. It was a typical totalitarian state building. One could hear the tango recordings coming from the basement. Shaking in fear, I looked for the room number in my summons. A long and narrow corridor of benches facing the offices and a uniformed policeman heightened my sense of panic and helplessness. Finally, after sitting on the bench for almost half an hour (the tangos kept going), the policeman opened the door and ordered me in.

When I entered there was a desk facing me. On the walls were pictures of Peron and Evita, and behind the desk was a sinister but elegant man, tall and slender with dark hair and a mustache, dressed in a gray suit, white shirt black tie and . . . riding boots. He said sharply, "Sit down!" I didn't know how to hide my anguish. I probably looked like a cadaver, but I made the effort and sat in the chair in front of him. He looked at my papers in a file and asked me if I knew "so and so." I said no, I didn't know him. He asked me if I knew that "so and so" was a member of the Communist party. Since I didn't know I responded accordingly, but my knees were shaking. He looked at the file and one more interrogation followed. Another name came up. "He was a classmate in high school." "Do you know that he is involved in subversive activities against the state?" was his question. I hadn't seen this fellow for several years and I had no clue about his political involvement. So I told my interrogator, "No, I don't know anything about it." *Kafka, the Gestapo, and the KGB are here*, I thought.

He continued with the questions like "Who is Alfredo Balparda?" I said that during my time at law school, Balparda had taken shorthand dictation and sold the mimeographed lectures of the professors to students who were unable to be present. The interrogator kept asking similar questions, and I started to relax. I realized that he was fishing, and since he couldn't prove that I was involved in any political activities, his tone became (at least in my imagination) a little softer. But you never can tell, and the climax of our interview dramatized that almost excruciatingly.

> *Interrogator:* You have asked for an application for a passport. What is the purpose of it?
>
> *Me:* I have been admitted to the Paris National Music Conservatory.
>
> *Interrogator:* Why? Don't we have a great many music schools in Argentina?
>
> *Me:* Of course. Had it not been for the qualifications of my teachers here I would not have been able to win the scholarship.
>
> *Interrogator:* So why do you want to leave the country?
>
> *Me:* Do you realize the honor it represents to have an Argentinean admitted to one of the most prestigious music schools in the world? I respectfully submit to you that this should be a cause for pride to our country![8]

He looked carefully at me and slowly opened his desk drawer. He pulled out the passport and proceeded to sign and stamp it. It already had the signature of the chief of police. "You can go now," he said. My heart was pounding but I tried not to run: after all, in the corridors of the Special Section the tangos were still playing.

Once in the street, I rushed to the bar where my friend was waiting. It was almost noon, and I had been in the horrendous building since 10:00 a.m. We celebrated and then I walked home. Despite my joyful enthusiasm, I couldn't help feeling a little sad. The beautiful city of Buenos Aires, its parks and avenues and streets, when was I going to see it again? Now I had to face my parents and tell them that I was leaving. Memories flooded into my mind of our summers at the Atlantic resorts, my trips to the Patagonia, the lakes, the Andes. Such a wonderful country, prisoner of a suffocating regime. I was going to miss my family and friends, but as Borges wrote in *The Death and the Compass*, "The first letter of the name has been pronounced."

Coda

Should I Have Sold My Soul to the Devil?

I always loved to read. Even as a child, authors like Jules Verne, Defoe, Emilio Salgari, and H.G. Wells took me to places and on adventures that, in a way, were anticipating my own destiny. Even in grammar school, I devoured the books of history and geography in the first days of the school year. Perhaps I needed to dream about new horizons in time and space. My imagination was vastly stimulated, and perhaps this is one of the secrets of my impossible mission.

As I grew up and became a teenager, always searching for role models (Igor Stravinsky, Dizzy Gillespie, Arnold Schoenberg, Charlie Parker, and so on), I read Thomas Mann's *Dr. Faustus*. This book left such a strong impression on me that I read it many times, even memorizing several passages. In it Faustus finally achieves the discovery of a new musical idiom and the glory attached to his endeavor, although he has to pay a painful price for them.

Schoenberg and Stravinsky, whom by now I deeply admired as exemplars of new music, helped the author with technical advice; the context and thrust of the book also made me think of Gillespie, Parker, Monk, and the other musicians who were changing the face of jazz. How to find a musical idiom that would integrate all these different streams of history? The idea of a composer who sells his soul to the devil in order to find a new musical idiom appealed to my growing questions about the creative activity. Of course, I did not wish to make deals with the devil—to this day I do not believe in the Prince of Darkness—but I did accept the idea as a poetic image because it was (and remains) frightening and enabling in equal measure.

My decision was made about exploring the relationships of different sounds among themselves, of penetrating the density of the chords, and investigating the possibilities of rhythmic combinations. A firm determination started to crystallize about my future in music. It was not an ambition, but rather a need to learn, discover, and expand my musical horizons. Though the world outside with its conflicts, coup d'états, and rigid dogmas mattered very much to me on one level, it did not impinge on my need to explore the fragile path of unknown answers to my questions.

Perhaps I was lucky. Perhaps I was at the right place at the right time. But what followed was a persistent obsession that became the secret of those answers. I owe my relative success to my avid curiosity, and also to the legacy of the old masters and what I've learned from the new ones.

Notes

1. Richard Palmer adds: "My mother had an analogous experience with one of her earlier piano teachers, a rather ferocious lady who barked out instructions without taking time out to be sure that the student had understood them. One such was the mysterious command, 'Hammer calm!' My mother did her best to obey what seemed to be a requirement to pulverise the keys in as serene a manner as possible—not very easy, if not indeed impossible! Only later did it transpire that the teacher's reference was to a 'hammock-arm'—i.e., addressing the keyboard with the arms deployed in such a way as to resemble the curve of a hammock. The metaphor is in fact a good one to describe the pianist's recommended physical attitude, but like all metaphors it needs to be understood before it can be acted upon!"

2. Flora is now a professor of Latin American literature at Columbia University in New York City.

3. This was so successful that six months later I was also responsible for the Argentinean premiere of the *Concerto in F*. I was twelve years old.

4. Recently, the Alumni Association of the CNBA granted me a merit award. Unfortunately, I was unable to attend the ceremony, but I sent a message thanking them for the honor. One of the paragraphs contained the following thought: "In order to be a composer and an orchestra conductor, one must know history, languages, mathematics, humanities, physics, and chemistry."

5. See the coda to this chapter—"Should I Have Sold My Soul to the Devil?"

6. Gulda's repertoire was impressive. Equally at ease with Bach and Mozart, he also recorded the whole cycle of Beethoven sonatas.

7. There are further thoughts on Borges's genius in chapter 6.

8. I meant what I said, but his jingoistic mind interpreted the superpatriotic overtones of my statement.

~

CHAPTER THREE

Fugue

fugue: From the Latin for *flight*. In music, a fugue is a polyphonic work for two or more voices or instruments that develops, by contrapuntal means, a subject or motif.

As I departed from Buenos Aires for Paris on the French ocean liner *Claude Bernard*, all the passengers began to scream, "Peron, son of a whore!" Flight may be angst-filled, but it can also be wonderfully liberating.

The head of the travel agency upgraded my ticket to first class with the condition that I should play piano after dinner for one hour, which I accepted gladly. Among the passengers were eighty-five young ladies from the French College of Superior Studies and the Alliance Française. Their male counterparts were seven young men, including me. I thought about a science fiction story of a society where females are prevalent and men are slowly disappearing. The rest of the passengers were older. We just knew that we were going to have a good time—and we did.

However that first night, before going to sleep, I could not help but miss my family. I was aware of their sadness, but our links were so strong that the distance could not affect our love. And in the evenings at sea—the stars as a ceiling, the excitement of exploring new lands, and above all the feeling of adventure invading all of us—those eighty-five girls and seven boys created a feeling of friendship and camaraderie. It was inevitable that some love affairs should develop during the voyage and that jealousies and conflicts among the girls took place; in retrospect, though, everything was amusing.

Geography came to life. We visited the ports of Rio de Janeiro, the Canary Islands, Dakar, and Lisbon; finally, after a journey of eighteen days, we reached Bordeaux.

We went by a bus provided by the travel agency to Paris, where history now came alive. While preparing all the logistical matters (contacting the Music Conservatory, searching for living quarters, and a host of other things), I walked and walked through the city, up and down, to the point where I had almost memorized the topography.

My first living quarters were at the university's city dorms. The food was pretty bad and there was no privacy. I needed to live alone, so I went to a hotel on the Left Bank frequented by jazz musicians.

Life in the Conservatory was quite functional, but one could feel time's density. Berlioz to Debussy to Ravel and Boulez: I felt the satisfaction of joining their legacy. But I had a lot to learn and lots of work to do—and in the former respect, a professor's remark to one of my classmates was crucial: "I never find any mistake in what you do. Yet I wish sometimes I *would* find a mistake, but also some beauty."

I remember a girl from Venezuela who was an extraordinary pianist. Her father was a very wealthy oilman who gave her a substantial allowance to get started in Paris. We would go to her place every evening. She had bought a nice flat near the Trocadero and also a brand new Steinway grand piano, but that cleaned her out—she had no more money and there was no furniture. A group of students brought food, and there was always somebody cooking for all of us. While walking through the long, large, empty apartment, one could open the door of a bathroom and find a young man practicing the cello; I did my harmony and counterpoint exercises in the kitchen. The domestic setup was not *quite* as bad as *La Boheme*, and it was certainly colorful, if one could ignore the cacophony of different instruments being practiced in all places and from all directions.

I got the offer to work in an elegant nightclub with a Latin dance music band and to write arrangements for the band. The pay was good and I was able to get my own apartment right on Boulevard St. Germain near the Metro Odeon. But my need to play jazz was an obsession. I had sat in several times at the Club St. Germain, and eventually I was hired by one of the best European musicians at the time, Bobby Jaspar. A Belgian, he was a virtuoso tenor saxophonist, a flutist, and the leader of great quintet. This was my first opportunity to play jazz as a professional musician and in the best circumstances.

In these new, invigorating circumstances I was anxious to sever my connections with that Latin band. But this proved very difficult, and indeed nasty. For a start, I was vulnerable in that I had only a student visa and was not allowed to work, making me easy prey for any vengeful blackmailer. And the band's leader (who had been born in Uruguay) turned out to be just such a creature. Originally, he had commissioned me to do Latin arrangements for the band, and he liked them so much that he also offered me the piano spot in his outfit. I told him I did not have the time. But when he found out that I was playing jazz at the Club St. Germain, he denounced me to the police because I did not have a work visa. The police came to my apartment, and they "accompanied" me to La Cite (police headquarters). They asked many questions, and I realized I was in a different situation: not only did I not have the work visa, but their main curiosity was how did I make a living? Since I was paid cash, they suspected that I was involved in illegal activities.

I asked them to come with me to my place and showed them ten compositions published by Eddie Barclay, who gave me a big advance for them. (It was the first time I was paid as a composer.) They seemed satisfied on that matter but, nevertheless, they told me that I could not play the piano in nightclubs or theaters, and if I did, I would be expelled from France.

It is difficult to express my desperation. To play the piano and write orchestrations was essential in order to survive but also to keep making progress in the field of jazz. Obviously, I was reaching new horizons at the Conservatory, but, in order to feed my genuine personality, it was imperative to continue my collaboration with the European musicians with whom I was nursing my jazz vocation.

Fortunately, I moved in different circles as well, and luck came to my rescue. A top career diplomat from the Argentine Embassy (not a Peronist) had connections with the French government. After a few days, he told me that if I played a recital in an auditorium for a big celebration of young students, the Minister of Education would be there and she would be willing to advise me on what to do. I went along: the place, on the outskirts of Paris, was huge, and thousands of students attended. I selected a repertoire including the Three Preludes by Gershwin, the Argentinean Dances by Ginastera and "Le Tombeau de Couperin" by Ravel. Afterward, the great lady (whose name I cannot remember!) Minister of Education came to my dressing room to congratulate me and thanked me for participating in the concert. She gave me a card with an appointment with the Minister of Labor for the following week.

Needless to say, I was very punctual for the rendezvous at the Ministere du Travail. His Excellency was waiting for me and gave me the work permit without any restrictions, providing me with a permanent resident visa in France. When I left the building in Place Fontenoi, the birds were singing and the sun was shining.

And the good news kept coming. As I mentioned before, a music publisher, Eddie Barclay, was interested in ten of my compositions, for which he gave me a substantial advance. Now I could claim that I was a professional composer as well as a practicing pianist, and I decorated the apartment in celebration.

On the French music scene I observed two parallel revolutions. The first was jazz-centered—traditional musicians versus the be-boppers, a conflict that led to riots and fist fights. (On occasion, I was afraid that they were going to march on La Bastille!) The second took place in the Conservatory, where the avant-garde students of Olivier Messiaen were united against the post-romantics, and several other factional disputes, including the post-serialists, who espoused the ideas of Anton Webern and thereby dismissed other postwar contemporary schools of composing. Pierre Boulez said, "Schoenberg is dead: we must burn all the opera houses." Nadia Boulanger, one of the most respected composition teachers, declared, "In the German post-romantic school there are three 'hysterical' composers: Richard Strauss, Anton Bruckner, and Gustav Mahler."

In the middle of these separate but related commotions, I tried to preserve my sanity. That was not easy, for two reasons. First, I had very little time to get any sleep between my music studies during the day and my performances at night. Second, my co-musicians were similarly divided, and obdurate too. I invited several classmates to accompany me to the Salle Pleyel to listen to Oscar Peterson; I told them that aside from extraordinary piano technique, he had harmonic and rhythmic ideas worth paying attention to. They said, "No, that's jazz: we're not interested." At more or less the same time, I told my fellow jazz musicians that during our next night off there was going to be a Ravel Festival at the Opera. I pointed out some similarities between the modern jazz harmonic progressions and the composer's, who had been a lover of our music, especially evident in his *Piano Concerto in G* and his *Violin Sonata*. "No, that is long hair music" was their response.

I felt doubly a stranger. From that point on I decided to keep my mouth shut and enjoy all kinds of music, using only my subjective taste as a guideline. Word went around the Conservatory that I was playing jazz at night. Olivier Messiaen, whom I revered (and still do), was the professor of analysis and composition, and his mind was one of the most brilliant I ever encountered. He opened my ears to new perceptions of music; he created a new musical idiom dividing the octave in equal parts originating scales, which melodically and harmonically postulated a different aural dimension. His theories about the duration of sound were a turning point in the music of the twentieth century, although he had based them on his studies of Hindu and

African rhythms. Pierre Boulez, Luciano Berio, Karl Stockhausen, Luigi Nono, and Ianis Xenakis had been his students.

He was disappointed with me when he found out that I was a jazz musician. He did not understand the articulations of this music around the weak beats of the measure, so he could not get the feeling of swing, which is surprising for someone who had a deep knowledge of African rhythms. Messiaen said to me, "How can you play music with constant-pedal rhythm?"[1] I remember what Louis Armstrong and Duke Ellington said about jazz: "If you have to have it explained to you, you won't get it." I regretted his character change toward me. But, as long as I was doing the right homework for him, he respected me. And I multiplied my efforts to show him that my extracurricular activities by no means diminished my obligations to his class. [Many years later, in 1997, while on a promotional tour for my film score *Tango*, I met one of my fellow ex-alumni, Michel Fano, in Paris. He said to me, "Maitre Messiaen was always proud of you and said marvelous things about your work for him." "Then why didn't he say that to me when he was still alive?" But perhaps he was still around.]

Messiaen was a mystic and a devout Catholic. He played fabulous organ improvisations in the Church of the Trinité during Sunday morning mass. Sometimes, on Saturday nights my fellow musicians in St. Germain would make social plans after the gig. "Don't count on me because I am going to mass," I said. They looked at me as if I were crazy. The fact is that I grew up in Buenos Aires in a religiously mixed family: Jews and Catholics intermarried. On Saturday nights my father would sometimes take me to temple. On Sunday mornings I would go to mass. All this was confusing to me since I was observing different rituals for the same God. Therefore, I embraced no religion at all, but grew up believing in a universal God. I could not accept that the Supreme Being could be so petty as to demand worship. Also, it was difficult for me to believe that He, like an accountant, would keep tabs on each one of our acts. However, that helped me to build an inner sense of personal responsibility, and my general moral values coincided with religious ones.

One night, during one of our breaks at the Club St. Germain, I went around the corner to the Café de Flore, where I knew Jean-Paul Sartre and Simone de Beauvoir were sitting at one of the outdoor tables with some of their followers. Sartre said, "If God exists or doesn't exist is not my problem, it is His problem." Some time later, being so antiestablishment, he rejected the Nobel Prize in Literature. But one of his disciples, who was more radical than Sartre, said to me, "The problem is not to turn down the prize, the problem is not to deserve it." Sartre, who was a prolific writer, created novels, plays, essays, philosophical studies, and screenplays. Among them was one called *Le Diable et le Bon Dieu* (*The Devil and the Good God*). When it was time for me to return to the Club St. Germain I abandoned the theological discussion, which continued. People like me had been standing around the existentialist thinker's table and continued there. The irony is that the Café de Flore is across from the Church of St. Germain des Prés, the oldest in Paris.

Once back in the club, I went to the bandstand and joined the quintet. We all noticed that at the front table was sitting a gorgeous blonde lady. Bobby Jaspar, our leader, looked at her with sensual intensity. She fixed her eyes on him. He called for us to play a ballad medley and was seducing her with his saxophone. His tone became very erotic, and she was responding to his love calls with an ecstatic expression. The ballads kept going until the end of the set. When we finished, he paid her check and the two of them disappeared into the street. We went to the bar and the drummer asked, "Where did Bobby go?" "He probably took that blonde to his place," we responded. "Oh no! She is not a woman but a man, a transvestite!" We did not believe the drummer because he was a practical joker. In the middle of the next set, Bobby appeared, alone and disheveled, with an expression of infinite fatigue. Afterward, we all went to the bar and asked him what had happened. He said, "She is great, one of the best times I've ever had." "How is that possible? Jean-Louis said that she is not a woman, she's a transvestite from Pigalle." Bobby's face started to contort in horror, and his whole expression became one of disbelief. "Come on, couldn't you tell?" we asked. "She said she had her period and couldn't make love in a normal way!" was his answer.

He immediately proceeded to get absolutely drunk; we did not know what to do. We followed him outside the club, and he walked toward the Seine River. He was so shocked and disgusted that he wanted to commit suicide; he was determined to jump into the black waters. He suddenly had supernatural strength and we could not do anything to stop him—until another Belgian musician, a vibraphone player, Sadie, who had just finished working in a nearby club, Taboo, appeared from the shadows. He was big and strong and saved Bobby Jaspar's life. We never broached the subject again. I thought about Sartre, Messiaen, and the Church and couldn't help but think that perhaps this was the devil's joke. . . .

Another religion I was exposed to during my time in Paris was the animistic cults of Africa, but I did not learn about them from the members of the colonies that France possessed in the sub-Sahara. Around that time, an influx of Afro-Cuban musicians, singers, and dancers came to the French capital. Their music had become very popular all over the world. Everybody was dancing the mambo and the cha-cha. It was of great interest to me; first, because of my curiosity about ethno-musicology, and second, because of the association of Dizzy Gillespie with Chano Pozo and Charlie Parker with Machito. So I learned Cuban music through the Latin jazz door.

I became friends with this new influx of people, whose roots were the same as those from which jazz was derived. A singer, Oscar Lopez, told me a story that ignited my curiosity about his beliefs as well as the life of an important figure of this new music. Chano Pozo was a Cuban virtuoso of the conga drums. In New York City, during the mid 1940s, Dizzy Gillespie was so impressed with his musicianship that he decided to incorporate him into his modern jazz band. But Chano also had another instrument, the bata, which is a cylinder of carved wood with skins on both extremes and, with the help of a leather strap, hangs from the neck and lies horizontally, unlike the conga drums, which are fixed to the floor vertically. This particular instrument came from Africa and was passed down through Chano's family for many generations. It is a ritual drum, and it is not allowed to be used for commercial purposes.

However, in a recording session with Dizzy's band, he not only used it but also sang a religious chant from Africa on the famous suite *Cubana Be-Cubana-Bop*. As soon as the record was released, his family in Havana decided to disown him for having desecrated their beliefs and committing apostasy. This excommunication consists of laying out the effigy of the one who was the object of punishment in a coffin. The funeral starts and everybody cries because the person is "dead" to the members of the family and the sect. This service takes place during one week, and at the end of the week the coffin is entombed under six feet of earth, like a real internment.

Meanwhile, in New York City, he had a serious incident with two Puerto Rican drug dealers. Unfortunately, Chano Pozo was a cocaine addict. He accused the dealers of cheating him and selling him a low-quality product; not only that, but he insulted them in front of their girlfriends. [Meanwhile, the Havana "funeral" was continuing.]

Chano's friends warned him that these dealers had sworn to kill him. "I don't care about those sons of bitches," he said. Toward the end of that week, he had to fly to Baltimore with his regular conga drums, in order to play a concert with Dizzy's band. Upon his arrival at his hotel, he found out that the skins of his congas were broken. He flew back to New York immediately, for in East Harlem he knew an old blind Cuban man who changed the congas' skins. He told Chano to come back in a half an hour and they would be fixed by then.

Chano Pozo went around the corner to a bar on upper Fifth Avenue. He put "Manteca" on the jukebox, which he had cowritten and performed with

Diz. While he was standing with a drink listening to the music, the two Puerto Rican dealers shot him through the bar's window and killed him. [At that moment, in Havana, his coffin was descending into the effigy's final resting place. . . .]

My connection with Cuban musicians opened a new source of income in Paris. RCA France hired me to arrange many albums for French bands, which incorporated the Cuban rhythm sections into their formations. Besides which, I could speak French to the wind players and Spanish to the percussionists.

To this day, I cannot fathom where I found the time to study at the Conservatory, play jazz at night, and work on arrangements and compositions for publishers and record companies in the mornings before breakfast! My social life had also started to become very demanding, and like a chameleon, I was moving in different circles aside from my classmates and jazz musician friends. French society is very peculiar because of the country's history; there is the Bourbon's nobility, the Napoleonic descendants, and the high bourgeoisie. For some reason I became very popular with all of them. In addition there were my Latin American friends, most of whom were studying at the Sorbonne. Some of them earned a living by playing Inca music in a Latin Quarter club called La Scale. Then there was the diplomatic corps, interwoven in all those circles.

I met Albert Camus and one of the ex-models of Henri Matisse's at a particular party. Prior to his arrival, there was a lottery among the young men present. I was not allowed to participate, and it was explained to me why: they had all had intimate relationships with one of the girls and she had become pregnant. Since in those days the DNA test had not yet been developed, it was a matter of honor to marry her, and this explained the lottery. The winner was congratulated effusively. This was the strangest engagement party I had ever attended. When Camus arrived with Matisse's ex-model, he was in a somber mood, not too talkative because he had just been at the funeral services of one of his best friends. I couldn't help but think about his famous novel, *L'Étranger*. Another one of the invited participants was a surrealistic poet who, a few days later, took me to the house where Modigliani and Breton had lived.

In 1954, I was invited to participate in the Paris International Jazz Festival at the Salle Pleyel, representing Argentina. There was an article about it in the *Paris Match*. I remember arriving backstage with my bass player and compatriot, Ricardo Galeazzi. I went to my dressing room, which had my name written on the door. To my surprise, once inside I saw and heard none other than Thelonious Monk warming up at the piano, totally oblivious of his surroundings.

In 1955, after winning my first prize in composition at the Conservatory, I decided not to go for the Rome Prize[2] and stayed in Paris. Of course in the summers I participated in jazz concert tours all over France. I learned how to appreciate the French cuisine, the wines and the cheeses that had originated in each region. Since France was occupying some German border states, we played for the French troops in Sarrebruck. In Baden-Baden, I could not help thinking that nine years before, the Nazi hierarchy was enjoying the resort and its casinos.

In September 1955, Peron was overthrown and had to find refuge in Paraguay. My parents and sister called me, jubilant! The streets of Buenos Aires were filled with excitement and celebrations. After four years without being with my family, I decided to return for a short visit. There was not room in my plans to abandon Paris, where I was now so well established. I was dying to embrace and kiss my mother, my father, and my sister, to be with my friends and get the feeling of Buenos Aires without Peron. I reserved my return ticket for March of 1956.

My last concert before my journey took place in the French Riviera during one of the worst winters in history. Ice and snow were in the Mediterranean Ocean, covering the palm trees. An arctic cold froze the air. It was, however, beautiful and picturesque. My fellow musicians and I went for a walk before the concert in Cannes. An attractive lady was walking her dog near the Hotel Carlton. We stopped, smiled at her, and she smiled back. She had been a member of the Ballet of Monte Carlo, and she was a dance instructor. Although she was about ten years older than I was, I invited her to our concert. What I did not tell her was that at 2:00 a.m. I was getting the train to Paris. I had to abandon the town in order to make my preparations for my trip to South America. She came to the concert, and afterward I wanted her to have a drink, which she thankfully declined. What was I going to do if she accepted?

The whole gang came to the train station to say "Au revoir" and wish me "Bon voyage." The next day, the telephone rang in my Paris apartment while I was packing. It was the ballerina, who was very upset and conveyed her anguish. "I met your colleagues this morning, who told me that you decided to leave France because you felt rejected by me. Believe me, I didn't know that you were so in love with me, and I confess that when I heard you playing the piano I felt very touched by your sensitivity. I think that, despite our age difference, I feel very attracted to you. Please reconsider, and if you come back to Cannes please ring me up. This is my telephone number. . . ."

I had to avoid my smile even over the telephone. My friends had pulled a prank that was a little cruel, but funny. So this was the way my first visit to the land of Voltaire was coming to an end. I don't remember her name, and our paths never crossed again. In musical terms, this fugue ended in a suspended cadence, because its continuation was my anticipated return to Argentina.

Notes

1. He meant the walking bass, which for him, no matter how much it moved, always stayed in the same place, according to his concepts about the elasticity of sound duration.

2. Rome Prize—The Paris Conservatory has a mansion in Rome where the winners of the composition first prizes can stay for one year and write a major work, like a symphony or cantata.

~

CHAPTER FOUR

International Incidents #1—Paris

1954: Chet Baker in Paris

In 1954, the famous American trumpet player Chet Baker left the Gerry Mulligan Quartet and formed his own group. He came to Paris to perform at the Salle Pleyel. After his concert, he visited the Club St. Germain where I was playing with the Bobby Jaspar quintet. Chet Baker decided to sit in with us, and we all played a jam session. He called for a tune titled "What a Difference a Day Made" at a very up tempo. When it came his turn for a solo, he liked the way I was accompanying him, very percussive and staccato.

He had a French lady friend, very sensual and pretty but with an aura of danger. She had a "vamp" personality and knew she was attractive, but the danger was always around her, like an invisible veil. She had big dark eyes surrounded by an intense and menacing shadow. Her lips were thick and her lipstick very dense. Her makeup was far from being subtle. There were no straight lines in her voluptuous body. She was certainly very attractive, but she radiated a sort of negative magnetism.

On the other hand, Chet was warm and effusive. He told me he was very impressed by my playing and especially the way I played behind him, supporting his combinations of highly fast passages with lyrical ones.

A few days later, the dangerous vamp called very distressed: Baker's pianist, Richard Twardzik, from Boston, Massachusetts, had died of a heroin overdose, and the quartet had to continue their European tour. "I must talk to you," she said. She came to my place and told me in a very seductive way that Chet wanted me to be his pianist. She was practically offering herself to me if I accepted. It was difficult to resist the temptations—her body and Chet's fame. But I knew he was, like other members of the group, a drug addict: that was the biggest danger of them all. And I had prepared all year for the exams at the conservatory, and I did not want to drop out. So I turned down her double offer. Naturally, they found another pianist, and that evening I knew at what time the train with the whole group was leaving for Germany. I started to hit my head against the wall, not knowing if I had made the right decision.

Anyway, today not only do I not regret it, but a few years later I would be a member of the orchestra led by another international famous trumpet virtuoso: Dizzy Gillespie.

During the next few days I went through the tests and won first prizes on fugue and orchestration. And on the weekend, I joined my French jazz musician friends. We were hired by the U.S. Army, which has headquarters in the vicinity of Paris. After all, this was happening only nine years after the Second World War ended. An army bus picked us up at L'Arc de Triomphe. The leader was a Yugoslavian bass player who had more success as a PR man with the American Embassy than with his instrument. He was so bad that my colleagues and I asked him not to play, and among all of us we shared a fraction of our fees to pay for a good bass player, Eddie de Haas, who was born in Holland. The Yugoslavian didn't seem to care; while we played he hopped from table to table and fraternized with the base commanders. I remember that on Saturday we played for the officers and on Sunday for the troops. And I can add a significant culinary detail: while living in Paris I was exposed to the best and most delicious treats that the French cuisine can offer. At the American Army base I discovered a new delicacy: the hamburger.

Some years later, I had the opportunity to reencounter Chet Baker. We were both playing at the San Remo Jazz Festival with our groups. Another star was Romano Mussolini, a great Italian pianist whose father had been none other than the infamous Italian dictator, Benito Mussolini.

After the concert, there was a reception that we all attended. Chet wanted to approach Romano to tell him how much he enjoyed his playing. But, as he got close to him, he said, "Man, what a drag about your old man!"

Paris, April 1955

A world famous Peruvian singer, Yma Sumac, was appearing at the Olympic Theatre. She had an extended range, from deep contralto to an extreme double soprano tesitura, which was the secret of her success. Yma Sumac was traveling with her own group of musicians, which included an extraordinary conga drummer. The manager of the jazz club Ringside, which later was to become the Blue Note, was so impressed with him that he invited me to the Olympia to listen to him playing. I also thought he was outstanding. After his performance we were introduced. His name was Dave Rivera, and he was Puerto Rican. I liked him immediately; he was humble and a little shy.

The Ringside offered me the opportunity to form a quartet (bass, drums, Dave on congas, and me on piano). We had to perform the following week, as that was the only time Dave was free before continuing on the European tour with Yma Sumac. The following Monday afternoon we had a rehearsal. During the break Dave told me that he lived in New York City. He showed me pictures of his family and his fiancée, with whom he was looking forward to getting married. They were in love, and the wedding was planned to take place upon his return to New York.

Jazz fans in Europe had not heard Latin jazz since Dizzy came with Chano Pozo to Paris, and that evening was a great musical experience for both me and Dave, who deservedly got a standing ovation. But the following evening Dave was extremely agitated and distracted. During the break, in his Puerto Rican English and broken Spanish, he told me his predicament. The previous night after the gig, he had gotten drunk and went with a French prostitute. The moment she found out he had an American passport, she kept him in the hotel the whole night, and in the morning she took him to the Municipality of Paris, where she forced him to marry her. The prostitute wanted to go to the United States and he was her ticket; naturally, Dave was extremely worried about his fiancée in New York.

I tried to comfort him and told him that it would be easy, under the circumstances, to get an annulment. But he said that he found out that under French laws, in those days, it was impossible to get a divorce once a judge had signed the marriage certificate. The next day, through my connections, I found a French divorce attorney who spoke English as well as Spanish. He charged Dave a fortune, but he promised he would try. He needed character references about the new wife. How could I help? I certainly did not know her, and I certainly didn't know who her pimp was. All of a sudden, a miracle! Dave tracked down her mother, an old French lady who happened to despise her daughter, her profession, and her ingratitude. The mother was willing to testify against her own daughter. They went to court the following day, and the divorce was granted.

Dave was beside himself with joy and invited me to a celebration at the old lady's apartment. She was going to cook for us. I was reluctant to accept but felt sorry for the guy and we went. The old lady was leading us into a God-forsaken part of Paris. We had to walk up seven flights of stairs. When the apartment door opened I perceived a strange smell. I love animals, but her cats were looking at me with a menacing attitude. I tried to eat the old lady's meal (she was a fairly good cook) and toasted Dave's freedom with a mediocre wine. The cats kept slowly coming at me, especially the one that looked extremely mean. I hurried through the meal and said to Dave, "Tonight is the last night at the Ringside, and we must go now." I was thinking to myself, "What am I doing here, why did I have to go and get involved in his problem?" But he had such an innocent look that I was inclined to forgive him. Finally, the formal thanks and farewells were exchanged. And just as I was about to shake hands with our pathetic hostess, the evil cat attacked me! I panicked, trying to protect my hands and face until I was finally liberated from the vicious creature. That evening I dreamed that I had a feline personality and that I was looking at the world with an unusual intensity. Perhaps I was destined to write "The Cat" for Jimmy Smith ten years later, perhaps I became a cat . . . somebody was pouring milk on my plate. . . . Anyway, that was my April in Paris, or rather my "Tiger Rag."

~

CHAPTER FIVE

South American Genius I—Music

Brazil and Bossa Nova

The first time I went to Brazil I made an excursion through the Amazon River and arrived at Manaus. The famous opera house in the 1950s was one of the most surrealistic monuments in art history. It was founded at the turn of the twentieth century by the rubber barons. When they left Manaus (rubber had been replaced by synthetic materials), the opera house was abandoned and slowly was invaded by the surrounding jungle. When I visited, the structure was in place, but the old red velvet golden seats had deteriorated to an indescribable dark color, baptized by moisture and bitten by erosion. Plants were all over the inside of the theater, and iguanas were running in what was left of the aisles and the boxes *avant scene*. The theater was remodeled in the nineties, but the memories and echoes of that encounter will always remain with me. Similarly evocative was a fort near Guyane, Cabedelo, which made me think of Africa. I could hear chants at night accompanied by drums, and I could see people staring at me through the windows of their huts.

However, before I came to the United States, I played with my band in Rio de Janeiro during Mardi Gras (Carnaval). The first evening after our concert, we went to a restaurant where musicians hang out. We arrived around 1:00 a.m., and before we could order our meals, the dancing crowd entered the restaurant, which had outdoor tables like many similar establishments, especially in Paris. When the dancers discovered the band's instruments at our large table, they practically kidnapped the musicians, who were forced to march through the streets of Rio. Luckily, as a pianist I did not have any instrument and they left me alone. After the supper I went to the hotel and tried to sleep. The music in the streets continued, and at six o'-clock in the morning my first trumpet and Gato Barbieri knocked on my door, completely exhausted but happy. However, we did not go back to the same restaurant the following nights.

In the early sixties, I returned to Brazil with Dizzy's band. We played concerts in Rio, Sao Paulo, and other places in the mountain resorts. Diz became fascinated with the rhythms, which were different from the Afro-Cuban ones with which he was so familiar. We went to the Rio de Janeiro outskirts, and he recorded with one of the samba schools. Unfortunately, the spontaneous session was done outdoors, and the sound quality was not good enough for an album release. But we had a good time anyway.

It is known that Gillespie refused to play jam sessions because his playing was so intimidating that the other horn players put their instruments back in their cases and left humiliated. However, in Rio and Sao Paolo I took him to the club where Jobim, Bonfa, Gilberto, and other experts of the bossa nova were performing. He brought his trumpet not to impress anybody but to learn the tunes. *Bossa nova* means new sound, and it was a cool derivative of the samba. The jazz influence on Brazilian musicians gave place to a new cross-pollination. I made some arrangements, which we recorded on an album, *Dizzy at the French Riviera*, that was released a few months later than the Stan Getz sessions for Verve.

Creed Taylor asked me to arrange an album for Luis Bonfa and also to make two of my own—one with Bob Brookmeyer, *Samba Para Dos*, the other *Piano Strings and Bossa Nova*. [I also recorded another one, *Brazilian Jazz*, with Leo Wright.][1] All these excursions into Brazilian music led to my participation in the first international bossa nova festival at Carnegie Hall, organized by the Brazilian Consulate in New York. Stan Getz and I were the only non-Brazilian musicians, who included Antonio Carlos Jobim, Luis Bonfa, Joao Gilberto, Sergio Mendez, Baden Powell, and Oscar Castro Neves.

Some years later, one of the greatest slow samba ballad singers, Maysa Matarazzo, "the Ella Fitzgerald of Brazil," showed up in Los Angeles. She had been married to the Count of Matarazzo, who had a very bad reputation: they used to call him the Marquis de Sade of Brazil, and apparently he corrupted Maysa and taught her a lot of sexual perversions. I dismissed all this as rumor, so when she asked me to introduce her to record and film producers, I gave a dinner party in my house, inviting several important Hollywood people including Jack Lemmon, Peter Falk, Stuart Rosenberg, and their wives; Ray Brown also joined me both socially and musically. After the meal we all went to the living room, and by this time Maysa Matarazzo was so drunk that not only could she not sing, she also started to make seductive passes at the men and their wives! ("Let's go to the bathroom and make peepee together.") I have never been so embarrassed in my whole life, but this incident did not affect at all my love for Brazil and it's music.

Tango

Buenos Aires, my hometown, is the last South American capital of the vast continent, which faces Africa. The different migrations of European descendents have made a mark on the city of boulevards, avenues, tall buildings, opera theaters, concert halls, movie theaters, restaurants, museums, parks. There is Avenida de Mayo, which is a replica of Madrid's Gran Via. The railroad stations had been built by British companies, and it's almost like being at Victoria Station in London. There is a neighborhood not far from the Pink House (presidential offices) that remains as one of the last examples of the Spanish Colony. The African slaves used to live there, but this Argentinean Harlem, called San Telmo, has narrow cobblestone streets and now has become a very fashionable antiques store district.

At the turn of the twentieth century the upper class hired French architects and urbanists, and the north section of the city looks like the Sixteenth Arrondissement in Paris. Italian immigrants were especially prevalent in a River Plate's port neighborhood called La Boca, which reminds you of Genoa and Naples. Buenos Aires looks at the Atlantic Ocean, and Borges said that it is not a real city but rather a dream. And being born and growing up in a dream contributed to my European formation and my fascination with jazz, which was born in another city of dreams, New Orleans. Moreover, visiting Argentina's interior offers you an awesome kaleidoscope of lights and shadows from a historical past, which lies in its geological crib: the Pampas, an ocean of green land; the Patagonia, the ancestral environment of Nomadic Indians; the Andes; the lakes; the northeastern jungles; the northwestern provinces, which were the last confines of the Inca Empire.

The music of Buenos Aires is the tango, which reflects the different European migratory streams. In my early years my father forbade me to listen to tangos on the radio. He considered them vulgar, and their origins were in the houses of prostitution. As I grew up I also rejected the commercial tango of the Peron era, especially the lyrics, which were always about some guy who was abandoned by a woman (usually a call girl). Nevertheless, the old tango, which had come from African influence, attracted my curiosity. And the new tango of Astor Piazzolla and Horacio Salgan was part of the same movement that created virtuosos on the bandoneon.

This instrument, which was invented in Germany in the early Renaissance, is a sort of portable organ and was used in small churches that could not afford a large instrument. How is it possible that the bandoneon became the sound of the tango as the saxophone is for jazz? From the little churches to the bordellos to the dance and concert halls—that is one of the strangest musical journeys in history. Astor Piazzolla came to Paris while I was at the Conservatory and asked me to play in one of his first records in Europe. I asked him, "Why me?" and his response was "Because you swing, and my kind of tango has to swing."

Horacio Salgan is a pianist who must be in his early nineties. I discovered him at the same time I'd gotten my first modern jazz records. He has an incredible technique and his musicianship as a performer, composer, and arranger is impeccable. There are three pianists in the Americas: Oscar Peterson in jazz, Chucho Valdez in Cuban music, and Horacio Salgan in tango. When I went back to Buenos Aires in 1996 to write and record the music of Carlos Saura's film *Tango*, I suggested that Salgan should be included. And Saura was so impressed by him that he gave him a whole shot in the movie, not only as part of the background music but visually as well. The musicians say about Salgan: "This son of a bitch never makes a mistake!"

Piazzolla hired me as a conductor in 1990 to perform and record his *Concerto for Bandoneon and Orchestra*. After the session, which took place at the auditorium of Princeton University, I went with my wife, Donna, and the head of the record company to a Cuban restaurant. Astor had traveled all over the world and was a gourmet, but he did not know Cuban cuisine. We sat down and ordered and were chatting happily—he said how pleased he was with the recording, and I then recounted my visit during the break to the university's physics department, where Albert Einstein had developed his theories about the universe—when all of a sudden, Astor remembered how vilified he had just been in Buenos Aires by the traditional tango musicians. In their opinion, his music was not pure tango (remember Diz and Bird?). Astor became very upset, and since he had a volcanic character, the whole culinary experience was about to be ruined. At that point I said, "Astor, who cares if your music is tango or not? Your music is pure Piazzolla." He started to calm down, gave us a smile, and proceeded to enjoy the food.

I have also made my own explorations in the world of the tango: *Three Tangos for Flute, Harp, and Strings*; the second movement of my *Piano Con-*

certo No. 2 ("The Americas"); one movement of my "Homage a Ravel" (for piano, violin, and cello), and the compositions for the film *Tango*. Recently I wrote a piece for the Chicago Symphony, which was performed in 2004: *Fantasy for Screenplay and Orchestra*. The "Love Scene" is very seductive, almost erotic, and embraces the tango rhythm.

On the other hand, the Gauchos from the Pampas perform a dance called the malambo, which definitely has African rhythms. The malambo helped my understanding later on of the music of Machito, Chano Pozo, and Chico O'Farrill. It also led to my final movement of *Gillespiana*, "Toccata." I also made occasional travels to other countries in Latin America. Montevideo and Punta del Este in Uruguay bring warm memories from my childhood (I've had summer vacations with my parents and my sister). Later on with my band we played concerts in Uruguay. Also the Jazz Club of Montevideo organized jam sessions, which were a lot of fun.

Finally, two codas. In 1970 I went back to Rio: a Brazilian choreographer had created a ballet for my *Jazz Mass*, which I conducted. The performance was televised, and the following evening I was invited to Ipanema, a beach community nearby. To my surprise the most fashionable restaurant, where I had a wonderful dinner, had an enormous discothèque designed as a replica of the biggest country in South America. And all the walls were covered with . . . my *Schifrin-Sade* album! Talk about cultural exchange!

In 2005, on my return from a tour of Australia, I participated in a very unusual event. I was commissioned by the Lincoln Center Chamber Ensemble to write works based on Argentinean music. Apart from wetting my feet with Carlos Saura's film *Tango* in 1998, I had not done anything of that sort for a long time. I was a little reticent about the whole thing, especially because I had to play as well as conduct, and the combination of chamber music, tango, and Argentinean folk music made me a little bit apprehensive. I didn't give myself too much room for improvisation.

However, the results were beyond anything I expected. The ensemble consisted of a sextet in which a distant cousin of mine, David Schifrin, played the clarinet; Jimmy Lin the violin; and Nestor Marconi the bandoneon (he came all the way from Argentina). Pablo Aslan was on bass, Satoshi was on percussion, and I played piano. Both concerts were greeted with standing ovations, great reviews, and enthusiasm. We went on tour in the summer with the same program, which included the Santa Fe, New Mexico, festival, and also recorded *Letters from Argentina*. Mind you, I will have to be careful that Astor Piazzolla's fans don't seduce me into exploring their territory even further, because I might be abducted!

Following are my program notes for the concerts.

Letters from Argentina

Like the clear sky, like the rain, like the clouds, music has always been part of the Argentinean atmosphere. The strumming of the Gauchos' guitars, the rhythms of the Indian drums, the expressive melodies of the bandoneon, were the aural medium in which I grew up. In Argentina, the music was ever present in the literature, in the visual arts, and in the history of the country.

Tangos coming from radios, folk music sang and danced in festivities, Milongas and Candombes celebrating Mardi Gras surrounded my childhood in Buenos Aires.

Letters from Argentina are the musical memories enhanced by my imagination and converted into impressions of my homeland. Working on this project helped me to recreate an unreal past in which a memory persists and invites us to a journey full of promises and dreams.

Note

1. A fine flutist and alto saxophonist who was in Dizzy's quintet for several years and one of the many stars of *Gillespiana*.

~

CHAPTER SIX

South American Genius II—Jorge Luis Borges

In 1995, I was commissioned by the Eaken Piano Trio to write a work for them. A piano trio as known in the classical world is constituted of a violin, a cello, and a piano. Because Maurice Ravel has written one of the most memorable piano trios, and since he is one of my favorite composers, I decided that my composition in four movements would be titled "Hommage a Ravel."[1]

The members of the Eaken Piano Trio are based at the Dickinson College in Pennsylvania. They alternate their master class activities with their concert tours and recordings. I sent the music in advance so they could have ample time to rehearse the work before the world premiere. I was supposed to attend the concert as well as participate in a seminar along with a question and answer session. On the way to Dickinson with my wife, while at the Los Angeles Airport bookstore, I picked up a book called *Borges the Poet* edited by Carlos Cortinez. Jorge Luis Borges has been one of the most influential personalities in my formation, along with Bud Powell, Igor Stravinsky, Dizzy Gillespie, and Bela Bartok. I've mentioned earlier my brief encounters with him in Buenos Aires, and my reverent attendance of his lectures. But something almost eerie happened on the way to Pennsylvania. Once seated on the airplane I opened the book, and to my surprise, it consisted of a series of lectures plus questions and answers that Borges gave at my very destination, Dickinson College, nine years earlier in 1986!

Jorge Luis Borges was a great poet and was also known for his unusual essays and short stories. His points of view, the angles from which he observed

the universe, eternity, and infinity, are original and enlightening. Borges refused to write long novels because he said that once he came up with the raw
concept of a story, he was too lazy to develop it. Why use unnecessary de-
scriptions or pedantic ornaments when directness and simplicity are the very
core of the style?[2]

Of course, Borges was also a poet. He commanded many of the leading European languages, and he was versed in Sanskrit, classical Greek, Hebrew,
Latin, and the old Anglo-Saxon as well. Since words are instruments of
thought, his vast knowledge of history, literature, philology, and philosophy
helped him to express his ideas in the most profound, economical, and simple way possible. He was a candidate several times for the Nobel Prize in Literature, but he was never granted the award. Perhaps his political ideas, an-
titotalitarianism, and unconditional opposition to the extreme right or left
(he openly showed his displeasure with Fidel Castro) were not well received
in Stockholm.

During the flight I devoured the book, and upon our arrival, I showed it
to the members of the Eaken Trio. They knew about Borges's visit nine years
earlier, which had made a big impression on the Dickinson College faculty
and students. Another surprise awaited me. We were taken to the guesthouse
where Jorge Luis Borges had stayed, and we slept on his bed! A similar experience took place in Iceland a few years later in which we stayed in the same
hotel as he did during his visits to Reykjavik. The mysteries of the Vikings
and Icelandic sagas were one of his passions.

After the Dickinson College "Hommage a Ravel" performance and after
my lecture, I met the members of the faculty, who warmly remembered
Borges's visit. They were enlightened and challenged by his thoughts. One of
them gave me a large photograph of Argentina taken by a space satellite: in
true Borges fashion, the point of view is different from the standard cartog-
raphy. One can recognize the contours of the Southern cape of South America in every detail, but it is upside down!

This incident, like many others in this book, could be interpreted as paranormal; I prefer to think it a coincidence. But one must admit that the mathematical odds of something like this happening are not high. My attitude
about it is to follow Placido Domingo's words: "I am not superstitious because
it could only bring bad luck!"

When I attended Dizzy Gillespie's funeral at a Catholic church in New
York City, obviously many generations of musicians were there to pay their
respects. From Milton Jackson to Wynton Marsalis, we were all grieving for
our tremendous loss. Since Dizzy had been a member of the Baha'i faith, and
Lorraine Gillespie, his widow, is a Catholic, there were many Baha'i clerics

and priests as well. The ritual eulogies started, and all of a sudden I was asked to say something as well. My first thought was, "Who am I to talk, in front of all these theologians who are more experienced in these ceremonies and probably know more about the afterlife than I do?"

Nevertheless, the following words began to flow from my mouth: "Dizzy's music is known for its angular and asymmetric lines. Perhaps those were messages from God that are left up to us to decipher. He has left a legacy to all of us which is also a responsibility to continue and expand his ideas."

The same encomium applies to Borges.

Notes

1. The "Hommage a Ravel" has been recorded by the Eaken Piano Trio for the Naxos label on a CD: *Schifrin-Schuller-Shapiro*.

2. The literary equivalent of Anton Webern and Thelonious Monk—very few notes but the right ones.

PART II

FROM GILLESPIANA TO JAZZ MEETS THE SYMPHONY

CHAPTER SEVEN

~

Gillespiana

After an absence of four years, Buenos Aires was as I'd imagined Paris to be following its World War II liberation.

I had intended my visit to be short; I was still planning to return to France and had kept my apartment along the Boulevard St. Germain. A few days after I arrived back, though, I received a telephone call from the new head of national radio and television for Argentina, an Italian married to the daughter of our new vice president. He invited me to his office and said he'd held a similar position with the RAI in Rome; he was a jazz fan and wanted to establish a jazz big band as he'd done at RAI. He said he'd heard I was coming back and so had waited for me, having interviewed other Argentinean arrangers, none of whom had convinced him as potential bandleaders. Suddenly, therefore—and I was not even twenty-four years old—I was being offered my own orchestra, with the added dimension of radio and TV programs! At that time, Gato Barbieri was still playing straightforward be-bop tenor saxophone just like Gene Ammons, Dexter Gordon, and Sonny Stitt. We made our debut two months later with great success. The band had four trumpets, four trombones, five saxophones, and a rhythm section. I was conducting from the piano.

And then something even more special occurred: my long-standing jazz idol was about to arrive! From my late teens onward, every time I left the house I would say to my mother, as a joke, "If Dizzy Gillespie calls, tell him I'm not here!" But now he was materializing, the real flesh-and-blood Diz. It seemed like a fateful encounter: my return from Paris and his tour were on two converging lines!

He played in a Buenos Aires theater for the whole week, and it was sold out. I went to every concert and we met. During that week there was a reception for Dizzy, his wife, Lorraine, and the whole band, and I was asked to perform with my own band for them after the dinner. He heard my piano playing and my arrangements. Immediately after we'd finished our set, he came up and asked if I'd written all of the charts. I said, "Yes," and his response was "Would you like to come to the United States?" I thought he was joking. Perhaps they called him *Dizzy* for a good reason! But, no, he meant it.

It seemed, however, that the State Department was less keen for me to take up his invitation. American bureaucracy meant that I waited two years before getting my green card from the United States Consulate in Buenos Aires; I finally arrived in New York City on September 28, 1958. But even then I couldn't get a work permit from the American Federation of Musicians because of *their* own rule, and I had to wait almost a further year to be able to play piano with a regular band.[1] I was allowed to write arrangements and to play as a replacement pianist, though. Xavier Cugat was preparing a new nightclub act for his singer, Abbe Lane, and I wrote all of the arrangements, became the musical director, and even did a symphonic album for Cugat himself (RCA). But I was still aiming to work with Dizzy Gillespie. . . .

After gaining my work permit, I formed my own trio, which played once a week in three different New York clubs: the Hickory House, Basin Street East, and the Embers. Meanwhile, I was calling Dizzy without any positive results. In those days there were no answering machines, and Dizzy didn't have an office. Eventually, one night he was performing at Birdland, and I went to see him. He said, "Hi, I heard you were in the U.S.—so why didn't you call me?" I said I'd tried, often. Anyway, Dizzy asked me: "Why don't you write something for me?" So over the weekend I composed the sketches for the *Gillespiana* suite. On Monday evening I went over to his house and played them for him. He asked me how I was planning to orchestrate it. I said I'd like to do a kind of *concerto grosso* for his quintet, surrounded by Latin percussion and brass orchestra, in which I would substitute four French horns and a tuba for the five saxophones of a standard big band. Right in front of me, he telephoned Norman Granz, the founder and then still head of Verve Records. Dizzy asked me how long it would take to orchestrate the suite. I estimated about two to three weeks. So he asked Norman to book a studio in one month's time. Just like that!

I started work immediately. But about one week later Diz called me to say, "I've some bad news." My heart fell: I thought he meant he wouldn't be recording the piece after all. Instead he said that pianist Junior Mance was leaving his group. Recovering slightly, I said: "Do you have someone in mind to replace him as pianist?" His answer being "I was thinking of you . . . ," I almost fell off my chair. The very idea that my first major piece, composed for a giant on his own turf, was not only going to be composed, arranged, and conducted by me, but I would also play piano for it!

When I arrived at the recording studio I felt very nervous, because not only was Diz there, but also such jazz stars as Clark Terry, Ernie Royal, Urbie Green, Gunther Schuller, Julius Watkins, et al. who were in the band. Still, the recording went well, and there was a lot of excitement. Gunther Schuller brought John Lewis along the next evening, and they signed the work to MJQ Music Publishing. The piece became very successful with both critics and the public. Dizzy got a gold disc and Norman Granz organized a world premier concert at Carnegie Hall, which sold out; after that he sent us on a tour all over the United States and Europe. I remember when we played at the Palais des Sports in Paris. At the end, Bud Powell came up to the stage to congratulate me. I had never met him before, and he was one of my idols as well as being the chief influence on my modern jazz piano playing.

I stayed on with his quintet from 1960 until late 1962. Playing with John Birks "Dizzy" Gillespie was immensely good for me spiritually—one of the happiest periods of my life in terms of music. It was very fulfilling to play with one of the giants of jazz all over the world, and to learn from him as a human being too. And there was never any end to my association with him. Even after I ceased touring with him on a regular basis, we were seldom out of touch and he was never far from my thoughts. Real friendship had intermingled with my admiration for his musicianship. And, of course, I continued to compose for him.

As so many are aware, one of his greatest gifts was the power of his humor. One night, around late 1960, we were performing at Birdland when George Shearing came in with his wife and a group of friends. They had a table close to the bandstand. I told Dizzy I wanted to meet him, because—like Bud Powell—he'd been an early idol. When we'd finished our set, I sat beside him and said it was an honor to meet him. Then Diz came over and told him he couldn't stand hypocrisy and, as a good friend, he had to tell him the truth: "George, you are black—but you didn't know it!"

In 1970 the mayor of New York gave the keys of the city to Dizzy. I was invited to take part in a gigantic concert that reminded me of a psychedelic time machine. There was a big band to play the early repertoire of his *Things to Come* period. Then I had the pleasure of playing alongside two of the greatest drummers of all time in quite separate quintets: Buddy Rich and Max Roach. All of the periods of Dizzy Gillespie's career up to that point were represented—and all of the participants around me that night were giants of modern jazz.

I've often said that I've had many teachers, but only one master: Dizzy. And I mean it—now more than ever before.

Note

1. George Shearing, another immigrant to the United States, titled one of his compositions *Local 802 Blues* after the NYC branch of the union!

~

CHAPTER EIGHT

A Dizzy Gillespie Miscellany

MacDizzy

Arriving at the Glasgow train station from London, the first thing that Dizzy Gillespie did was to stop people in the heart of Scotland: "Can you please tell me where the Gillespies live? You see I am a member of their family. . . ."

An American in Paris

While playing concerts at the Salle Pleyel in Paris, one late afternoon Dizzy and I went to a typical French bistro to have a drink. A big glass container on the counter, which contained a great amount of hard-boiled eggs, intrigued the great trumpet player. He observed the customers open the container and, taking an egg, break it and spread on some salt, chasing it with a beer. I told him that this was an old French tradition, like an abbreviated version of the Spanish "tapas," which are more elaborate and varied.

The next afternoon, Diz asked me to go back to the bistro. He was carrying a package. He went to the counter and when the bartender wasn't looking, Dizzy took eggs from the package and put them on top of the other eggs, quickly closing the glass top. He took me to a table and said softly, "Those are fresh eggs I bought at the market!" We ordered drinks and waited. The next innocent customer opened the top, broke an egg . . . and the contents started to slide over his hands and onto his jacket and slacks. It was a scene that Harpo Marx could have conceived.

However, once we were out on the street, Dizzy's expression was somber and he didn't talk for a while. Finally, he said, "I am sorry about what I have done. Everybody knows that I am a practical joker, but I always laugh with people, not at them. . . ." That evening we played *Gillespiana*, which was recorded live on the Europe 1 label on November 25, 1960. Dizzy's playing was outstanding. I think his clear phrasing was trying to erase the raw egg incident. Perhaps the victim was in the theater with a clean suit, enjoying the concert without suspecting that the person responsible for the prank was the very superstar facing him on stage.

Mistaken Identity

By pure coincidence, Count Basie's band bus stopped in front of the lobby of the San Francisco hotel where I was staying with Dizzy Gillespie and his band. At that moment, Diz asked me to hide with him behind one of the columns near the reception desk. Once all the Count's musicians finished the registration procedures and their luggage was taken to their respective rooms, my leader went to the information desk and asked for the room number of the trombonist, Benny Powell. Benny was an old friend of Dizzy's, and my mischievous leader went to the house phone and called him. I had no idea what was going on. Benny answered the phone, and Dizzy, using an impeccable falsetto, perfectly imitated a female's voice: "Hello, Benny?"

Benny: Yes?

Diz: This is Maggie calling.

Benny: Maggie? What Maggie?

Diz: Don't you remember me? From Boston? Don't you remember we had such a great time together?

Benny (still puzzled): Where are you?

Diz: Downstairs, in your hotel lobby.

Benny: Come on up, darling.

Of course, Maggie was a fictional character so Benny had no idea who "she" was. Diz told me to follow him. We took the elevator to the corridor of the ninth floor, where we found Basie's trombonist's room. Diz knocked at the door very gently.

Benny: Who is it?

Diz: (falsetto) It's me, Maggie.

We could hear the sound of a spray can and the smell of cologne coming from the room. Finally, Benny Powell, dressed in a seductive robe, opened the door.

Surprise, surprise! But he got mad and a switchblade knife appeared in his hand. He chased us all over the hotel, and we finally found sanctuary in my room, where I discovered that I could laugh at the same time as feeling the stress of being an unwitting accomplice to a prank that was totally alien to me. In spite of it all, I couldn't help but respect Dizzy, for when we were on stage, his musicianship was paramount, and he was a constant source of inspiration. Sometimes I forgot to play the piano, listening to his amazing solos. So "Maggie" evaporated from Benny Powell's and my own memories. . . .

The Charmer

When Lyndon Johnson was the president of the United States, Dizzy called me in Los Angeles from Washington, DC, very late one night. He said, "You won't believe this, but I just came back from the White House. When I was introduced to the president and his wife, I said to Mrs. Johnson, 'It's an honor to meet you, especially because your name is very important in modern American music.'"

Mrs. Johnson: Oh, really?

Diz: Yes, madam, you are known as Ladybird. Lady Day was the nickname of Billie Holiday, one of the greatest singers in our music. And Charlie "Yardbird" Parker was known as "Bird." He was one of the fountainheads of modern jazz. So you see? Ladybird, Lady Day and Bird!

Mrs. Johnson: I never thought of that!

To Be or Not to Bop

Dizzy Gillespie was doing a promotional tour for his autobiography, appearing on television and radio shows. Around that time, to my consternation, I read in the major magazines and newspapers that his wife, Lorraine, was divorcing him for some of the stories featured in the book.

I became very concerned because I knew both of them, and after the fifty years they had shared together, I was afraid that the stress of separation was going to be impossible for both of them to survive. With great anxiety, I called their home and Lorraine answered the phone. I told her about my concern, and I asked her, "Why now, after you have shared a life together?" She laughed and said that the rumor of their divorce was spread to the news services by Dizzy himself and was not true. "Hell," she said, "If I had to divorce him, it's not for what is in the book, but for what ain't written in it!"

Wolftrap 1987

A gigantic event was planned to celebrate Dizzy Gillespie's seventieth birthday at the Wolftrap venue, near Washington, DC. The concert lasted six hours (from 8:00 p.m. to 2:00 a.m.) and started with *Gillespiana*. (The all-star big band's four trumpets were Jon Faddis, Wynton Marsalis, Freddie Hubbard, and Arturo Sandoval; J.J. Johnson was in the trombone section, and David Amram was one of the French horns.)

It was followed by "Be-Bop: The Early Years," with Benny Carter, J.J. Johnson, and a rhythm section, including an Afro-Cuban cameo with Mongo Santamaria, Candido, and many other stars in the field. Then came the Dizzy Gillespie Quintet, where James Moody, Charlie Persip, Al McKibbon, and I joined the master. There was a Brazilian vignette with Flora Purim and Airto, and Oscar Peterson and Carmen McRae also participated.

Dizzy was in great shape and played the whole concert, including numbers with Oscar (an *a cappella* duet) and Carmen, where he accompanied her at the piano and then she sat at the keyboard while he played trumpet. He never took a break during the six hours.[1]

All the musicians, TV crew, and production staff were staying at the same nearby large hotel. My wife, Donna, was with me, and we invited my mother to be with us. After one of the morning rehearsals preparing for the concert, everybody had lunch in the hotel's sumptuous restaurant. My wife, my mother, and I were sitting at one comfortable booth. Dizzy was table-hopping, and when he came to us he put his hand on my shoulder and defiantly faced my mother, saying "He is *my* son!" My mother, who was blonde, petite, and still good looking, looked at Diz with her green-blue eyes for a while, and then she said, "You know, I don't remember. . . ."

Needless to say, "Mr. Hip" had been outdone by a little old lady from Argentina. He fell to the floor with laughter.

I know I gave my parents satisfaction, but I wish my father had been alive for this event. However, I am glad that I was at least able to offer the experience of this extraordinary concert to my mother, who hugely enjoyed it and kept talking to me about it every time I had the opportunity to be with her afterward, either in Los Angeles, New York, or Buenos Aires.

Frustrations

When I arrived in New York in 1958, after two years of bureaucratic efforts with the American consulate in Buenos Aires, I realized that Dizzy had given me his personal home phone number and asked me to call him as soon as I got to New York. Every time I tried to call him, he was always away on tour and I could not reach him at all. His wife, Lorraine, never answered that phone, which was his private studio line. Since I was not financially secure, I needed to find a job immediately. I did hang out with some jazz musicians that I met in Paris or Buenos Aires, but they didn't have anything going on. Billy Mitchell was playing with Basie, and most of them were either already employed or they weren't in a position to help me.

I did one or two nights at the Embers with Gabor Szabo, but that was not enough to pay the rent. So finally, some of my Latin friends recommended me to a Mexican restaurant called El Rancho. I still remember the name of the boss, Patsy Alvarez. The restaurant was on 48th Street near Broadway, on the Westside, and the atmosphere was quite sleazy. I had to play piano to entertain the clientele, and my repertoire had to be either *Granada*, *La Malagena*, *Besame Mucho*, or *Boleros*. They paid me weekly, just enough money to survive, and also, occasionally some of the prostitutes approached the piano with their "johns," who passed me a tip of about $5.00 if I played their favorite tune. You can't imagine how demeaning this was. Meanwhile, I had approached John Hammond, who was the head of the jazz department at Columbia Records. He was married to Benny Goodman's sister and belonged to the New York high society. Before my departure from

Buenos Aires, Friedrich Gulda had given me his coordinates and told me that he would recommend me to audition for his company. Unfortunately, since El Rancho was near the theater area, one night, John Hammond and his wife were walking by and they saw my name on the marquis. They walked in and heard me playing the horrible music, which I was obviously playing mechanically and without any enthusiasm. Needless to say, that was the end of my possible professional relationship with Columbia Records. He avoided me like the plague, and his secretary stopped taking my phone calls.

Finale: Goodbye Dizzy

For stony limits cannot hold love out.

      —William Shakespeare

The private funeral service for Dizzy took place in a Catholic church, St. John's on Lexington Avenue at 52nd Street. His widow, Lorraine, is Catholic; Diz himself belonged to the Baha'i religion from Persia, which is a Unitarian faith (the Baha'i believers have been persecuted and many of them killed by Tehran's ayatollahs). Leading the service was another jazz priest like Father O'Conner, but younger. You can imagine: not only Dizzy's family, but so many of his friends were there. Needless to say, it was one of the saddest days of my life. During the whole flight from Los Angeles to New York, I seemed to be in a daze.

By the time the service began I'd noticed several Catholic priests and many Baha'i monks in white robes and turbans. Then came the various eulogies, and suddenly Boo Frazier, Dizzy's nephew, came over and asked me to say a few words. Lorraine Gillespie wanted me to as well. I was thinking, "What am I going to say in front of all these theologians?" But then it came to me, exactly as follows: "Dizzy's music is known for its angular and asymmetric lines. Perhaps those were messages from God that are left up to us to decipher. He has left a legacy to all of us which is also a responsibility to continue and expand his ideas."

When they opened the casket, Wynton Marsalis played a traditional New Orleans lament for the dead *a cappella*, just as Dizzy himself had done at the funeral of another trumpeter, his cousin Charlie Shavers. I was shaken by the experience—and its drama. But I knew Diz wasn't in that coffin. He was already with Charlie Parker playing *Groovin' High*.

Notes

1. The whole thing was televised, and an edited version of the event has been released on video.

2. This is analogous to his stern but impassioned remark, "Jazz is too good for Americans."

CHAPTER NINE

~

The Verve Years and a First Marquis

For all the joys and education that were fundamental to my time with Dizzy Gillespie, by 1962 I was increasingly aware that I wanted to branch out, both as an arranger and a composer. The year before, Norman Granz had sold Verve Records to MGM Inc., and the label's new vice president and chief producer, Creed Taylor, indicated that (largely on the strength of *Gillespiana*) he would like to sign me up as an artist.

However, striking out on my own meant that I first of all needed a top-class agent whom I could trust. I'd had one offer already from Duke Ellington's manager. He said I ought to consider leaving Dizzy, and he would take care of my career. I don't remember his name, but he was a white guy and had a very flashy office in Manhattan. Also Martha Glaser, Erroll Garner's manager, said to me that she'd never managed anyone but him, but she might make an exception in my case. But I ended up, very happily, with the man who at that time was also managing organist Jimmy Smith and also Stan Getz.

I'd just finished a tour of the Midwest with Diz and the Ellington band— which meant champagne and caviar every evening in Duke's dressing room— and was all set to play in Europe again. At the airport I met an African American by the name of Clarence Avant. He asked me in a cool sort of way, "Did you write the *Gillespiana?*" I said, "Yes." Then he gave me his card and said to call him after I returned. I did, and his office was a little cubicle at Blue Note Records: compared with the two previous proposals, not very impressive. He asked me, "What do you want to do?" I said, "Make records under my own name. Then I'd like to go to Hollywood and write music for feature films and

TV." His response was: "That can be arranged." There was something about his self-assurance, coolness, and demeanor that I liked.

And my instincts were good. Not only did he fix the contract with Verve, he also got me my first two movies in Hollywood. He could have kept on being my agent, but he said he didn't understand the film world. Instead he went on to be a record industry tycoon, including as CEO at Motown, and today is the guru for all the leading black music producers and artists. We've remained close friends, and I owe him a lot.

As well as my own albums for Verve, I became the in-house composer and arranger. I did an LP with Johnny Hodges, one of the great voices on the alto sax and a mainstay of the Ellington orchestra. Then I wrote *The Cat* for Jimmy Smith, which became his first million seller on disc. The record also won a NARAS Award for the best original jazz composition of 1964. I worked with Stan Getz,[1] and I did a Latin album, *Samba Para Dos*, with Bobby Brookmeyer.

I was pleased with all those projects, but the one that gave me the most satisfaction, and was in some ways the most momentous as well, was *New Fantasy*, recorded over June 10 and 11, 1964, at Rudy Van Gelder's Englewood Cliffs Studios, New Jersey. I had a marvelous group of players: four French horns, five trombones, four trumpets, a tuba, one saxophone doubling flute, me on piano, plus guitar, bass, and drums. The trombone section was a "dream" team: J.J. Johnson, Kai Winding, Jimmy Cleveland, Urbie Green, and Tony Studd (bass trombone). The trumpets included Clark Terry and "the hard man," Ernie Royal, playing leads. Jerome Richardson played the tenor saxophone and flute. The late George Duvivier, that rock-like figure of sensible music, was on bass, and Grady Tate our driving drummer.

Although I didn't fully realize it at the time, this album was the next stage of my journey toward *Jazz Meets the Symphony*. It was performed by jazz musicians possessed of all-round musicality, but the actual musical content was by leading contemporary composers: Aaron Copland, George Gershwin, Duke Ellington, Heitor Villa-Lobos, Richard Rodgers, and Aram Khachaturian. The album's title track was written by Larry Green: previously unrecorded, the line was nevertheless familiar to thousands of radio listeners as the *WNEW Theme Song*.[2]

All of the pieces are known and popular, from Gershwin's *Prelude No. 2 in F* to Richard Rodgers's *Slaughter on Tenth Avenue*, his ballet from the show *Pal Joey*. But while being totally respectful toward my various models, in the orchestrations I set out to dress them in new clothes. In Gershwin's *Prelude*, for instance, I emphasized the blues feeling more, looking to create a latter-day cry for freedom and wider horizons. Villa-Lobos's beautiful melody from his *Bachianos Brasilieras No. 5*, which originally combined classic Bach with the folk music of Brazil, now had a touch of modern Brazil, the bossa nova, grafted on.[3] *Slaughter on Tenth Avenue* was done as a jazz waltz, and for *Slaughter* and also *The Blues* from Duke Ellington's *Black, Brown and Beige*, I took advantage of Jerome Richardson's flute being on hand: in the former I alternated him with screaming French horns, but for Duke's piece I concentrated on a more lyrical approach, with some revised harmonic settings. Finally, I had always loved Khachaturian's ballet, *Gayaneh*, for its musical pictures of the Russian steppes—with flashing swords, leaping boots, and swirling capes—and to suggest that in today's aspirant society those same blades might slash away at taboos and breaking psychological chains excited me as much as the music itself.

A little over a year later, Creed Taylor approached me with the idea of making a record that combined European music (Middle Ages, Renaissance, Baroque, Rococo, and the early "classical" period) with jazz. The concept appealed to me very much, and I proceeded toward it by writing some original material as well as paraphrasing and adapting attractive fragments by composers of those periods. For the sessions I hired players from Pro Musica, a New York institution that promotes early music, and I also booked several of the best jazz musicians on the scene. When they all came into the recording studio, they were bewildered! For instance, a lute player asked Grady Tate, who was setting up his drums, "Is this the studio where we are supposed to do the Lalo Schifrin recording?"

In any event the results were very satisfying, though Creed and I still didn't know what to call the album. But then I went to see, twice, the big hit show on Broadway, the *Marat/Sade*. It appealed to me tremendously, not just because of the personality of the Marquis but also on account of the "play-within-the-play" approach, which comes from Shakespeare and later Pirandello and other playwrights. The fact that De Sade couldn't control his inmate-actors was an idea of genius by Peter Brook—and thanks to him we suddenly had a title for the Schifrin/ Sade recording: *The Dissection and Reconstruction of Music from the Past as Performed by the Inmates of Lalo Schifrin's Demented Ensemble and as a Tribute to the Memory of the Marquis De Sade!* It was very well received by the public and critics.

Notes

1. This refers to *Reflections*, which Getz recorded in 1963; the album is discussed in more detail in chapter 15, section 5a.

2. Intriguingly, that title had been recorded in the very same studios just a month before (May 6) by Stan Getz, Bill Evans, Ron Carter, and Elvin Jones. But it was not included on the original LP configuration, whose release was delayed anyway because neither Getz nor Evans was happy with the results. Verve eventually issued it, still against their wishes, in 1973, but the *WNEW Theme Song* did not see the light of day until the full session came out on CD in 1988.

3. This composition also features on Schifrin's album with the WDR Big Band, *Gillespiana in Cologne* (Aleph 002).

~

CHAPTER TEN

Jazz Mass

> Man must pray in music and he must pray in freedom. He must be able
> to sing, even when he is in a group, the congregation.
>
> —Fr. Norman J. O'Conner

The multifaceted and mystical virtuoso Paul Horn (flutes and saxophones) approached me in 1964 with the idea of writing a "jazz mass" when Paul VI was Pope. Under his predecessor, John XXIII, The Second Vatican Council had decided to allow the Catholic mass to be sung in the original languages of many countries instead of just in Latin, so that it could be more accessible to modern congregations; in addition, the Vatican was open to the proposal of a jazz mass in English. So with the endorsement of Father Norman J. O'Connor, I was commissioned to write this work. I'd first met Father Norman in Boston, where he had a local TV show and was known as "the Jazz Priest." He helped many musicians who were drug addicts through his foundation, and I played several benefits to raise money for his cause.

Paul Horn was an RCA artist; a member of RCA's board was Catholic, too, so a recording was agreed to as well. As I've said, I come from a mixed religious family: on my father's side Jewish, from my mother's Catholic—although even in my father's family there were many converts to Catholicism. My aunts, they were taking me to mass on Sunday mornings, but sometimes my father would take me along to his synagogue on Saturday evenings. Enormously confusing! I saw a lot of people worshipping the same God, but with different rituals. However, the *Jazz Mass* interested me greatly: the idea of a dialogue between Gregorian chant and a jazz ensemble was very appealing.

The original recording took place in Los Angeles in 1965. Paul Horn came up with the brilliant plan for scheduling the actual sessions at midnight. The studio was dimly lit, and the experience was truly spiritual. Because of the length of the composition and the inclusion of *ad lib* solos, which extended beyond the functions of the ritual, the Church suggested that I call it *Jazz Suite on the Mass Texts*. The record proved hugely successful, and I received one of my four Grammy Awards for Best Jazz Composition of the Year.

Later I extended the composition and changed its orchestration somewhat, though I retained the original title. If the music is too long for the regular liturgy, nevertheless it is still in performance "a jazz mass."

The *Kyrie* interpolates an antiphony of Gregorian chants by the chorus based on the Dorian scale, with a jazz motif by the band. During the *Criste* section, the soloists make the musical commentaries on the pleas for mercy. The *Interludium* is an instrumental development of the previous statements in the *Kyrie*. In this new version there are collective improvisations by all the members of the band. The *Gloria* starts with a sense of affirmation by the choir and the modes of the early Middle Ages, this time sung in canon. The soloist again is in charge of the exegesis.

The *Credo* is truly aleatory. The choir starts singing (not talking!), with each one in the lowest pitch, as softly as possible. When they run out of breath, they go up in pitch and dynamics. The tympani provides the background, and more percussion instruments are added as the crescendo continues until a true climax of fervor and affirmation is reached.

In the *Sanctus*, the rhythms become more complex and the voices follow a technique used later on in the development of the Gregorian chant: *organum*, using parallel intervals of fourths and fifths. The *Prayer* has three sections: (1) a bass flute solo *a cappella*, (2) an organ solo, and (3) a condensed recapitulation of (1) by the bass flute. The *Offertory* allows the development of the *ostinato* motif by the rhythm section, which grows into the whole orchestra's participating. This time the soloists lead the "congregation" while the band adds its textures in a "free" form.

Finally, the *Agnus Dei* is based on twentieth-century modes almost as if, during the whole process of the mass, new notes are being added to the basic scales in order to create a different aural universe. These added notes are also used vertically, creating a new harmonic sense. As the last section of the mass, it synthesizes the ideas of the dogma with the hope that the Lamb of God's sacrifice was necessary in order to make our prayers heard for a better, more tolerant world where love reigns.

~

CHAPTER ELEVEN

Jazz Meets the Symphony #1

To be or not to bop.

—Dizzy Gillespie

jazz: A kind of native American music marked by a strong but flexible rhythmic understructure, with solo and ensemble improvisations on basic tunes and chord patterns, and recently, a highly sophisticated harmonic idiom.

symphony orchestra: A large ensemble of string, wind, and percussion sections for playing symphonic works.

encounter: The act or process of coming together; a joining.

It is possible that encounters are predetermined by fate. Perhaps some of them are compelled by necessity, or maybe they are due merely to chance. In any case, my *Jazz Meets the Symphony* is a testimony to the superimposition of two strong musical forces: jazz, which was born around one hundred years ago, and the symphony orchestra, with a lifetime of more than two centuries. As the new millennium unfolds, this music can be considered as a celebration of walls and fences coming down.

For there is an imaginary world, perhaps in a different dimension, where a street in Vienna intersects a street in New York City. Beethoven, Mahler, Ellington, and Gillespie are gathered around a piano in a tavern exchanging ideas, improvising, and sharing melodic patterns and chord progressions. They also tell stories, and once in a while a good joke provides a burst of laughter. More musicians arrive, slowly. Through a process of variations around a theme, two cultural heritages merge in a stream that runs through time. While they play, they are aware of their differences (which they welcome); at the same time they concentrate on their similarities. In creating *Jazz Meets the Symphony*, I have tried to articulate my own beliefs and values, reflecting my parallel activities in the classical and jazz worlds. I have never understood the building of walls and fences that separate people's ideas and music. And although *Jazz Meets the Symphony* evolved comparatively late in my career, it is in several respects a culmination, weaving together many different strands in my musical life and thought.

In jazz the major inspiration comes from within. But in a small group the interplay between its members creates a different reaction, which definitely affects their musical ideas. If we extend this concept to a big band at its best and in ideal circumstances, the external propulsion will affect the individual expressions. And if we extend it further to the symphony orchestra, it should be possible to create an analogous though different atmosphere, one which would inspire jazz players.

The combinations of orchestral textures are infinite and highly conducive toward that objective. There were, obviously, historical precedents by jazz musicians and arrangers experimenting with new timbres or adding string ensembles to their improvisations—Duke Ellington, Gil Evans, Charlie Parker's "With Strings," and Stan Getz's *Focus* album scored by Eddie Sauter. But a full-size symphony orchestra offers the whole palette of musical colors, which, if well applied, can expand enormously the horizons for the soloist and his composer/arranger.

Some time before, Dizzy Gillespie had asked me to write an orchestration of *I Can't Get Started* for trumpet and orchestra to be played at the Jerusalem Festival with the Israeli Philharmonic. On reflection, perhaps that was the real beginning of *Jazz Meets the Symphony*. We repeated the performance in Cannes with the Symphony Orchestra of Lyons, with Ray Brown on bass and Grady Tate replacing the original drummer in Jerusalem, Mel Lewis.

The concept for an entire CD combining both worlds came while I was making an album with Jose Carreras in Germany for East West Records, a subsidiary of Warner Bros. The head of the company, Jorgen Otterstein, was an admirer of my music from the various collaborations with Creed Taylor. I proposed the idea of *Jazz Meets the Symphony*, and he agreed. Our joint decision was to record with the London Philharmonic. Meanwhile, I'd decided to form a trio with Ray and Grady since there was no budget for additional soloists. We tested the whole repertoire with the Honolulu Symphony at Waikiki (rather like trial runs out of town for Broadway shows). I wanted especially to study the "choreography" of my moving between the podium and the piano as the scores required.

Before I left for London, I'd found out Dizzy was very ill. So it was with great sadness that I recorded *I Can't Get Started* and the *Dizzy Gillespie Fireworks* medley as parts of my first CD; more affirmatively, I thought it would be a legacy for other symphony orchestras to perform music by the finest masters of jazz. The members of the London Philharmonic were certainly excited, and the whole experience became extremely rewarding. Also, deep inside me, I knew this was only the beginning.

On my return I was eager for Dizzy to listen to the tape I'd brought with me of *Fireworks*: his opinion was very important to me, naturally. However, when I called his home, his nephew answered the phone and told me they were taking my mentor, my guru, my older brother to the hospital. He never recovered. He passed away a few days later.

~

CHAPTER TWELVE

Jazz Meets the Symphony #2 and #3

Few things have happened to me, and I have read a great many. Or rather, few things have happened to me more worth remembering than Schopenhauer's thought or the music of the English language.

A man sets himself the task of portraying the world. Through the years he peoples a space with images of provinces, kingdoms, mountains, bays, ships, islands, fishes, rooms, instruments, stars, horses, and people. Shortly before his death, he discovers that that patient labyrinth of lines traces the image of his face.

—Jorge Luis Borges

As mentioned elsewhere, during the summer of 1963 I found myself on the same ocean liner as Miles Davis, leaving New York Harbor on our way to Europe. The relentless forward motion of the ship was pulling us to the reflection of different shades of time on the crest of the waves. At dusk, near dinner time, we felt that our meditations were converging toward this melting horizon. I can't help feeling that *Jazz Meets the Symphony* is another point along this same journey, where the stars meet the dreams and a line of memories, images, days, and nights are converging toward a new horizon. . . .

Anyway, the artistic, critical, and sales success of the first *Jazz Meets the Symphony* CD led to a second, *More Jazz Meets the Symphony*, and then a third, *Firebird*—this time with the addition of Jon Faddis, trumpet; James Morrison, trombone and other instruments; and Paquito D'Rivera, reeds. Meanwhile, a European booking agent, Burkhard Hopper from Munich, became sufficiently interested to book us for a tour with the Münich Radio Orchestra. We played in several European cities and at the Montreux and Pori Festivals. Also, our friends in the London Philharmonic persuaded their management to set up a London concert at the Royal Festival Hall on a subscription basis. I could hardly believe that jazz was being so easily accepted on both sides of the fence. My wife, Donna, said, "Be careful what you dream because it will become a reality!"

Between the tours in Europe, the United States, and South America with *JMTS*, I worked hard to prepare the scores for our new recordings. Each of my ideas to render a tribute to the masters from different periods of jazz (Miles Davis, Fats Waller, Louis Armstrong, Charlie Parker, and so on) would prove extremely satisfying. Besides which I composed several original works and started to adapt pieces by other composers (Joe Zawinul, John Lewis, and Gil Evans) that I thought were conducive to an orchestral instrumentation. I even devised a new notation by using what in mathematics they call "irrational numbers" in order to make the whole orchestra swing. The classical musician could hardly believe it when they found themselves actually *swinging*!

Around the time we were recording these new titles with the London Philharmonic, East West Records was assigned by Warner Bros. to their Atlantic division, and the executive put in charge did not have a clue about what we were doing. So I acquired the original master tapes, and this became the actual birth of Aleph Records. There is a story by Borges, *El Aleph* (1949), that tells us of a point in the universe through which all events converge. Since most record companies didn't know how to categorize me ("Is Lalo Schifrin a jazz musician, a classical composer, or a film guy?"), the Borgean *Aleph* seemed a perfect name to cover my various expressive needs.

Moreover, a new producer, Wolfgang Hirschmann at WDR, Cologne, started to hire me on a permanent basis. I'd worked with him before in Dusseldorf, conducting and recording a "live" concert with Sarah Vaughan. His personality is different from Creed Taylor's, but he responds to my musical ideas with understanding and enthusiasm. The first thing we did for him and Aleph was the new version of *Gillespiana* with Jon Faddis and Paquito D'Rivera. These two, both being disciples and former playing colleagues of Dizzy's, gave us all a great personal rapport. Our next project was the extended, more elaborate recording of the *Jazz Mass* with Tom Scott as soloist.

However, the very first release on Aleph was *Film Classics*: my arrangements of favorite movie themes, from *Gone with the Wind*, *Casablanca*, and *High Noon* to *Doctor Zhivago* and *Raiders of the Lost Ark*. One thing that helped the company enormously was Clint Eastwood's agreement to license our release of a Dirty Harry anthology (*Dirty Harry*, *Sudden Impact*, and *Magnum Force*). Then Aleph became very active with soundtracks: *The Cincinnati Kid*, *Bullitt*, *Cool Hand Luke*, and so on. We're up to thirty CDs now, including five volumes of *Jazz Meets the Symphony* and more in the planning and preparation stages.

~

CHAPTER THIRTEEN

A Second Marquis

A few years ago, Verve Records decided to reissue my *Marat/Sade* CD in a new, limited edition; it sold out immediately. My wife, Donna, suggested I should therefore do a sequel. That's why it's called *The Return of the Marquis De Sade*, rather like the Hollywood B movies of the 1930s and 1940s (*The Return of . . .*, *Son of . . .*, *XX Strikes Back* and so on).

There was no intention of proselytizing the man, De Sade. I have read the book about him by Simone de Beauvoir, and I am not fond of his perversions, even though, believe me, I'm far from being a puritan. The reason for doing these recordings was entirely musical; I wanted, so far as I could, to simulate the ways in which the great masters of the Medieval, Renaissance, and Baroque periods improvised. This was never going to be more than approximate, because we don't have any exact idea of how they went about their improvisations; the nearest we come to registering this area of their work is in the *Goldberg Variations* by J.S. Bach. Goldberg was a Bach disciple who wrote a theme; the master improvised around it; and his disciple, Goldberg, took down shorthand of these improvisations. Then Bach retouched it—unfortunately—but anyway, we get some idea of his intentions.

So, to sum up, it should be clear that the individual titles of *The Return of the Marquis De Sade* are not programmatic. On the contrary, as you will gather, *Relaxin' at Charenton* and *A Night in Venezia* are plays on words of famous titles by Charlie Parker and Dizzy Gillespie.

CHAPTER FOURTEEN

~

The *Esperanto* Suite

This was, in effect, a commission to celebrate the new millennium.

In 1887, a Polish eye doctor, Lazarus Ludovik Zamenhof, created an artificial language that he called Esperanto. Its intention was to offer mankind universal speech. His efforts were not entirely without success: Esperanto is known in eighty-three countries, and more than 30,000 books have been published in translation. However, today, only two million people in the whole world can speak Esperanto. Perhaps one of the reasons for its limited success is that there has always been a universal language: *music*.

According to the Hindu mythology, the universe hangs on a cosmic sound so massive and all-encompassing that everything seen and unseen (including mankind) is filled with it. To the American Navajo Indians, music is an expression of harmony between man and the forces of nature. Music, for most of early mankind, came from gods or supernatural beings as a gift.

The perception of this evolving process inspired me to compose the *Esperanto* suite. Borrowing a format from the Baroque era, the *concerto grosso*, the work is written for a group of soloists: violin, clarinet, bandoneon, trumpet (doubling flugelhorn and trombone), jazz drums, Indian tabla, and African and Latin percussion. The group of soloists is supported by a jazz band, an ensemble of players, and two electronic keyboards.[1] I decided to give the six movements straightforwardly evocative titles—*Pulsations, Resonances, Dance of the Harlequins, Millennium Blues, Tango Borealis,* and *Invocations*—feeling that as soon as we started to play the piece, everybody would understand what I was trying to do. And they did: music doesn't need too many explanations.

I wanted to build the work around soloists from all five continents. Virtuoso French violinist Jean-Luc Ponty is at home with straightforward jazz, jazz/fusion, and African genres. He made a wonderful contribution. The Argentinean bandoneon player Nestor Marconi is considered one of the world's finest practitioners. I love his taste, his musicality. Australian trumpeter and multi-instrumentalist James Morrison is a diehard swinger. He's been a great interpreter of my music over the years. The eclectic American clarinetist Don Byron has feet in many musical areas; like African drummer Sydney Thiam, he has a decidedly "world music" approach. And tabla player Trilok Gurtu is a master of Indian rhythms: it is wonderful, but in another way entirely logical, how he understood my rhythms and could interpret them from a Hindu point of view. Finally, trap drummer Greg Hutchinson is just great: hard driving, yet subtle. He can play all the styles.

In short: there are so many great idioms, but here there is a unity. It's not just a potpourri. Everything feels organic and functional, encouraging all the musicians to give of their best. In my perhaps utopian interpretation of the world, this work symbolizes the possibility of a future in which the sounds of music, more than words, could bring universal peace, tolerance, and a real communication among the members of the human race.

Note

1. Editor's note: the *concerto grosso* format Schifrin describes here is of course that which characterises his definitive work, the original (1961) *Gillespiana*.

PART III

MORE JAZZ

~

CHAPTER FIFTEEN

Anecdotes and Vignettes

Duke Ellington

In 1961, a two-band tour was organized to play concerts in theaters and universities auditoriums in the American Midwest.

One of the bands was led by Duke Ellington, whom I had met in New York. The other was Dizzy Gillespie's, performing *Gillespiana*. The two leaders took turns opening and closing the concerts between intermissions. Counting all the musicians, road managers, librarians, and stagehands, and Duke's butler and the driver, we were forty people on the gigantic bus. On one Sunday during the tour, we had two concerts in Iowa: the first an early matinee in a theater in a town, the second an evening performance at Iowa State University. We finished the first concert around 4:00 p.m. and had to travel a considerable distance for the next, which was due to start at 8.00 p.m.

We realized that we needed to have dinner before, otherwise everything would be closed in the college town after the concert. The bus stopped at every restaurant on the road; when the owners saw so many African Americans, their reaction was always the same: "Sorry, we are about to close." We were getting frustrated, and I couldn't help but think about the injustice of bigotry and prejudice. Being the only "white" musician in the whole troupe, I finally said to the driver, "When we arrive at the next restaurant, do not park up front. Let me go in alone."

So when we arrived at the next eating place, I walked in and with the most charming smile I could paint on my face said to the lady owner and some waitresses, "We are musicians on tour. Do you have room for forty?"

She fell for it: "Sure, come in, you're welcome!" I went back to the bus and whistled in the bus driver's direction. "Fellows, come in!" They all jumped out and ran toward the restaurant. I'll never forget the faces of the ladies when they saw the faces of Cat Anderson, James Moody, Johnny Hodges, Ernie Royal, and all the rest, thinking they were a branch of the Mau-Mau trying to overthrow the government of Iowa!

Even so, I have good memories of that tour. I never missed Duke's performances: I was riveted by his sense of showmanship and, above all, his musicality. Also, he always invited Diz and me to his dressing room during intermissions to have caviar and champagne. He was acting as the Duke of Ellington!

Who would guess what came about three years later in Paris, where I had been sent by MGM from Hollywood to score a film with Jane Fonda and Alain Delon. Since I was writing during the day, after dinner I used to walk through the Champs-Élysées to a club, the Living Room, where Art Simmons, an American ex-patriot pianist, was playing every night. On one occasion, I met Cat Anderson and Sam Woodyard on my way to the club. "What are you doing here?" We hugged, celebrating the encounter. "We just came from the Orient, and at midnight we are recording the latest of Duke's compositions, *The Ceylon Suite*." My curiosity and admiration for the master's work compelled me to go to the session, which took place at the Barclay Studio on the outskirts of the French capital.

We arrived near midnight, but there was nobody at the place. Sam started to set up his drums while Cat was warming up his trumpet. Slowly more musicians started to arrive, and around 1:00 a.m. there was quite an animated group of musicians, but Duke was still not there. At 1:30 a.m., Johnny Hodges came through the doors and we shook hands.

Finally, Duke came with his entourage of admirers (including the critic Hugues Panassié, who wrote one of the most comprehensive biographies of the composer), and he established himself in the booth. He started to check the controls with the engineer while the band was tuning up. They played the beginning of *The Ceylon Suite*. The special voicing in the saxophone section mesmerized me. All of a sudden, one of the trumpet players interrupted the rehearsal and said, "With jet lag I am hungry, and I cannot play when I am hungry!" They had to send for food at that late hour. Half an hour later, he was at his stand, chewing, quite satisfied. Meanwhile, I went to the booth and asked Duke to let me see the score. I checked the saxophone section voicing and learned a new methodology concerning the harmonic texture of the band.

Then, after so much waiting, they proceeded to finally start playing the piece, which was marvelous! Suddenly, Johnny Hodges stood up and asked, very angrily, "Who stole my watch?" Duke continued to be like the Sphinx, immutable to the problems of everyday life. At that point I decided to leave, but when I was back in the United States, Duke called me to have a drink together with my manager and friend, Clarence Avant. He offered me the opportunity to write an album for him, but as in the case of Miles Davis, the project never came to fruition due to our different schedules and the fact that we lived in different cities.

Nevertheless, I never forgot that, several years before, when I was with Diz, Duke came into the club. We played one of Duke's early compositions, "The Mooche." During my solo, I paraphrased several of his works, and he smiled with a sincere expression of approval. I am sure that this experiment led me to write "Echoes of Duke Ellington" for the first *Jazz Meets the Symphony* CD. I could not have expressed my admiration and respect for his place in jazz history without quoting, juxtaposing, and coloring essential fragments of his own music.

Oscar Peterson

When Oscar Peterson walked into the club in Toronto, Canada, where I was working with Dizzy's band, I couldn't hide my nerves. He is the greatest jazz pianist of our time. Also, he is one of the kindest people I have ever met.

A few months later, we traveled together with one of the Jazz at the Philharmonic tours. I was driving Norman Granz crazy to get me places with pianos where I could practice in the afternoons, so during the concerts Oscar wouldn't "cut" me too badly. During the tour we had the opportunity to socialize. I remember the dinners we had in the different towns we visited, when we were often joined by Benny Carter, Diz, Ray Brown, and sometimes J.J. Johnson and Stan Getz.

Oscar's playing is mesmerizing. He is a perfect example of applying a stupefying technique to the service of meaningful musical ideas. And he also has a great sense of humor. Oscar and Ray Brown were always reminiscing about the pranks they used to play since the beginning of their collaboration together.

Many years later, when I was already living in Los Angeles, the Oscar Peterson Trio was playing at the Century Plaza Hotel's lounge. I attended the performance with a Canadian jazz critic, Gene Lees.[1] For the occasion Gene donned a pair of thick glasses and a hat. I went to the bandstand to greet

Oscar. He was very cordial and in a very good mood. I said to him that a Russian jazz music critic "Vladimir Gretchko" was at my table and wished to interview him for Moscow's *Pravda* newspaper. Oscar accepted, and in the dressing room, Gene spoke with a thick Russian accent. I noticed that Mr. Peterson was starting to feel uneasy and becoming suspicious. Of course, he had known Gene Lees for many years. They were both from Toronto, and Mr. Lees had interviewed him for *Down Beat*. When Oscar discovered the truth we all laughed and went to our table to celebrate.

As the years passed, and I decided to begin professionally conducting symphony orchestras, Oscar Peterson told me, "I've heard that we are losing you." "No way: once a jazz musician, always a jazz musician" was my answer. Not too long after that I was hired by Norman Granz to conduct a symphony orchestra and a jazz band for an Ella Fitzgerald concert at the Hollywood Bowl. I couldn't help thinking about the cycles of fate. The first recordings I heard of Oscar Peterson's were with Ray Brown, when I was a teenager in Buenos Aires. Then, while I was in Paris, I went to one of the Norman Granz concerts, and Ray, Ella Fitzgerald (by that time Ray's ex-wife), and Oscar were part of the troupe. The next day I had lunch with Benny Carter, who was also with Jazz and the Philharmonic and had invited me to his dressing room the previous evening. When I went to the hotel where they were staying, I saw Ray and Oscar and spoke briefly with them. A few years later, I was part of their troupe! And one of my most vivid memories is the brilliant keyboard runs, the control, and the wonderful taste that emanated from Oscar Peterson's personality.

JATP, Frankfort, Germany, 1962

Norman Granz was fond of finishing JATP concerts in grand fashion. All the wind players who performed in different settings during the evenings had to play together in a gigantic jam session. However, there were two or three rhythm sections on hand, so Norman decided at the last minute to coordinate them. He was not following any particular rotation. On one particular occasion in Frankfort, Germany, he chose Art Davis on bass, Jo Jones ("Papa") on drums, and me on piano. The alignment for the horn players was Benny Carter and Cannonball Adderley on alto saxes; Coleman Hawkins, Stan Getz, Don Byas, and John Coltrane on tenor saxes; Roy Eldridge, Dizzy Gillespie, and Nat Adderley on trumpets; and J.J. Johnson on trombone

Roy kicked off the closing number at a very fast tempo, and the solos were ebullient—full of energy, great ideas, cascades of notes, and screams and applause from the audience. Then it was time to feature Jo Jones, who was not only a great technician but also an accomplished showman. He knew how to use the drumsticks and brushes on the tom-toms, cymbals, snare drum, with his feet on the bass drum and sock cymbals and his face in the spotlight. His solo was so long that we left the stage and waited for his signal to come back, whereupon a traditional riff based on the "Indiana" chord progressions was played in unison by the whole troupe.

Finally we got to the last chord, which lasted quite a long time: indeed, it is difficult to describe what happened during it. Jo Jones was all over the drums; Coltrane, Byas, and Adderley playing fast arpeggios; Stan Getz playing melodic lines; Hawkins was imposing his sounds, J.J. Johnson his long notes; Benny Carter and Nat Adderley displaying gentle figures. But Roy Eldridge and Diz were competing for the highest note. Meanwhile I was doing loud tremolos on the piano with the pedal down while Art Davis looked very serious with his bow on the bass. I was unable to hear what he was playing in the middle of all the pandemonium. So the end came abruptly. There was nobody to conduct a cutoff, but a miracle happened: silence.

Standing ovations from the audience, so everybody felt good and we started to walk away from the stage. As we were walking to our dressing rooms, Art Davis, very upset (he is also quite tall) told Roy Eldridge (who was of a smaller frame), "Man, there are many notes in a chord, why did you have to pick mine?" Roy looked at him, disoriented, not having a clue what he was talking about. But I realized that it took Art Davis the length of the final chord to discover what it took Arnold Schoenberg a lifetime to postulate in his twelve-tone row theory. It was a territorially imperative matter.

By the way, this time Roy Eldridge beat Dizzy!

Sarah Vaughan ("Sweet Sass")

In 1961 I was asked by Roulette Records to write the arrangements for a Sarah Vaughan album. I was delighted with the assignment because I had been a great fan of her recordings since my Argentinean adolescence.

The diva came to my house a few weeks after the initial phone calls. Sarah brought with her the lead sheets of the repertoire that was going to be included in the project. She sat at the piano and sang while she was accompanying herself. I was astounded by her harmonic sense, which was like Dizzy Gillespie's. He also played the piano, and his way of voicing and handling the harmonic progressions was unique. I pointed this fact out to Ms. Vaughan, and she confirmed that, in effect, Diz had taught her the keyboard harmony at the time that they were both working with the Billy Eckstine Band.

I was working on several projects at the time, but this was such a great opportunity that I opted to focus on each song and decide what kind of orchestrations would give the best inspiration and atmosphere to surround her magnificent voice. Another telephone call from Roulette Records informed me that the sessions would take place in Chicago where she was going to be performing a few weeks later. Teddy Reig, the producer, and I met at the airport in New York and went on to Chicago. I wrote the last arrangements on the plane. The following day, Teddy Reig rented a car and we left from the hotel. Sarah, her hairdresser, and I joined him and proceeded to drive toward the recording studio.

As we were crossing one park, the police stopped us. Teddy got out of the car and talked to the officers for quite a long time. I was worried that we would be late for the session. Finally, Teddy came back to the car, and we asked him what the whole thing was about. He said that the policemen found it very suspicious that two white guys were in same car with two black ladies. They thought that the ladies were prostitutes!

When we arrived at the studio, the Chicago Symphony was waiting for the downbeat. A booth was set up for Sarah in order to isolate her from the orchestra for technical reasons. I had written some lines for her, especially for the endings of songs, and it was amazing how well she sight-read the music.

At one point during our rehearsing, I stopped the orchestra to address some interpretation details. When my baton indicated that they should take the song from the top, I looked at the booth and nobody was there. "Where is Sarah?" I asked. Teddy told me to go to the booth and take a look. What I saw was the biggest surprise of my life. Sarah was on the floor laughing at my accent, which was thickly tainted by my Spanish-French background!

Despite her mirth, the sessions with the symphony and a jazz band were successful. After the sessions, the four of us went to the Playboy mansion, the residence of Hugh Hefner, who offered us a nice and well-deserved dinner. And that's how Sweet Sass came into my life and filled me with joy and great satisfaction.

Stan Getz

After the first day of working on an album with Stan Getz, we decided to listen to what we had so far. Since we were recording thirty-two tracks, his pianist asked Stan if he could re-record his solo. "I think I could do something better. I'm sure I could improve it." Stan's response was "No, man, this is jazz and you had your chance! Think about it for tomorrow's tunes and try to play your best. In jazz, you have only one chance, and that's it!"

Stan Getz: *Reflections*

In 1963 Creed Taylor commissioned me to do an album for Stan Getz with voices. Despite his bad reputation and temper, I had always had a very cordial relationship with Stan and a lot of respect for his playing. When Creed Taylor called, I had just come back from a Norman Granz tour in Europe, where I played with the virtuoso saxophonist. One of the numbers we performed was "Spring Can Hang You Up the Most," and I created a full orchestral arrangement of the song for the album, which brought out Stan's most rhapsodic playing. Another thing that fired my interest in this project was the choice of "Early Autumn," which had been one of his classic performances with Woody Herman's band.

Creed brought a group of studio singers, and the experience was new and interesting for me. Stan liked very much a ballad I had written called "Reflections," which became the title of the album. Later on, Gene Lees put lyrics to the tune, and the song is called "The Right to Love"; it has since been recorded by Carmen McCrae, Peggy Lee, K.D. Lang, and many other artists.

The session was very pleasant in its own right and also a kind of time machine for me, renewing my acquaintance with some of Stan's earlier successes, which I then re-orchestrated for voices. It also became a training ground for a record I did some years later with Dizzy and the Double Six of Paris.

Quincy Jones

In June of 1956, during a South American tour with my band, I went to a record store in Montevideo, Uruguay, that carried the latest jazz LPs. I had been aware of Quincy Jones from reading *Down Beat* magazine. I also knew that he had been Lionel Hampton's band arranger when Clifford Brown and Art Farmer were members of that band as well. Two of the records I bought in Montevideo were arranged by Quincy Jones—one featuring Julian "Cannonball" Adderley, the other Carmen McRae—and his unique voicings and orchestrations were a revelation.

A few months later, he came to Buenos Aires with Dizzy Gillespie's State Department Band. Quincy was fourth trumpet in the section (Diz played in front, naturally). To hear in person one of his finest compositions, "Jessica's Day," was a particular joy. And when later we met for the first time, he was not only most cordial but when I asked him for the lead sheet of "Jessica's Day" so that I could write my own arrangement for my band, he immediately got music paper and a pencil and in less than one minute, he wrote it down. I still have his manuscript.

Quincy was curious about Brazilian music, so I played him some tunes by the father of the bossa nova—a Brazilian singer-composer whose stage name was Dick Farney (his real name was Farnesio Dutra e Silva). Farney composed great songs, beautiful melodies accompanied by interesting jazz progressions. He influenced Jobim, Bonfa, and Gilberto. Quincy was fascinated by his music, and in a way our relationship started as a sort of cultural exchange. A few years later in New York, we started to spend time together. We had several things in common. He studied in Paris after my return to Argentina. He had also worked for Eddie Barclay, the publisher who discovered Michel Legrand and got me my first break as a composer.

Years later, while I was living and working in New York City, Quincy Jones asked me to orchestrate one of my original compositions, "Lalo's Bossa Nova," for his 1962 album *Big Band Bossa Nova*, on which I also played piano. He was also in charge of producing a concert with Sarah Vaughan and asked me to play for her.[2]

For a while, our careers developed on parallel paths. We got assignments in Hollywood almost at the same time. We kept meeting in jazz festivals where we were both performing, or in Paris or London where, by coincidence, we were often staying at the same hotels. I remember in Paris, we had dinner with Billy Strayhorn, the famous composer and arranger and Ellington collaborator. It was a quiet restaurant by the Seine on the outskirts of the French capital, and we had a wonderful conversation about music and wines, which I will never forget.

After my return to the United States, Teddy Reig, record producer and vice president of Roulette Records, called me in Los Angeles from New York. "I would like you to write an album for Louis Bellson." For all my enormous admiration for Louis, one of the foremost virtuoso drummers in jazz history, I did not immediately jump at the offer. "Let me call you back," I said.

My instinctive reservations had to do with the fact that Louis Bellson had not only played with virtually all the bands, including Duke Ellington's, but also had his own band. In addition, he is a great arranger and composer, and the idea of doing what was clearly expected—just one more big band sound showcasing his drumming—did not appeal to me. But another concept did. I called Teddy back and said, "Yes, I'll do it—but I want to do it with strings. After all, Charlie Parker, Dizzy Gillespie, Chet Baker, and Clifford Brown did albums with strings." There was a silence on the line. Finally Teddy said, "Yes, but they were horn players." Then more silence. I kept waiting, and finally he said, "Okay, go ahead!"

I proceeded to write a very adventurous album, all original compositions. Unconsciously, my journey to *Jazz Meets the Symphony* was moving steadily forward. The title of the album was *Explorations,* and Louis played not only drums but also timpani, bass marimba, and exotic instruments from the Orient like lujon and boo-bani drums. Teddy was unable to fly to L.A., so he appointed Quincy Jones as producer. Louis gave great performances; he was really inspired by the challenge. Quincy was transfixed, and he did a superb job in the control booth. He kept asking me questions about the unusual instruments and asked if he could borrow my scores. The cultural exchange between us was still going on. Later on, he moved into full-time production not only of records but of TV shows and movies as well. He deserves the success he has achieved because of his tremendous drive, imagination, and above all his musicianship.

When I think about the first recording I heard of his, with Julian "Cannonball" Adderley, I cannot help but remember that in the 1970s, Adderley—who was a truly amazing altoist—asked me to write a piece for a recording he was doing with a symphony orchestra. I called it *Dialogues for Jazz Quintet and Orchestra.* After looking at the score, Quincy Jones told me that he was afraid that I was losing my sanity. But he praised me for my boldness. "Cannonball" wrote the liner notes, and he called me "the wild bull of the Pampas, for whom minor seconds *are* beautiful."

A Rose Is a Rose: Thelonious Monk

A new jazz club was going to open in Chicago, the Bird House. I went to the opening night. The Thelonious Monk quartet was featured. However, Charlie Rouse (tenor saxophonist), the bassist, and the drummer started to play by themselves because Monk was late. They called him at his hotel room, and he said, "Man, you are hanging me up!" Anyway, as a goodwill gesture, one of the waitresses put a red rose on the keyboard, to welcome the great pianist and composer. Finally, Monk arrived, and with a lot of vigor he ran to the piano. But the unexpected red rose disoriented him. He kept looking at it, first with a lot of suspicion, and then slowly warming up to it and finally taking it in his hands. He still had yet to play one note. Then he brought the rose to his nose and smelled it, showing that he enjoyed the aroma. He was smiling. Realizing that it was time to play, he gently deposited the rose next to his bench on the floor.

The audience was enthralled with the spectacle, but Monk got back to business, embarking on a long and great solo. When he finished, it was the bassist's turn, and all of a sudden, Monk stared at the rose on the floor. He stood up and started to do a sort of "Mexican sombrero" dance around the beautiful flower. Finally, he decided to come back to his universe and, realizing that the rose was disturbing the order of things, with a final heavy downward motion with his legs, he crushed it! Now, he had found peace of mind, and he proceeded to play a beautiful rendition of "Ruby, My Dear."

Miles Davis and John Coltrane

In the summer of '63 I became involved with Quincy Jones again. He'd been asked to produce an album for Phillips: *Dizzy Gillespie and the Double Six of Paris*. As usual, he was up to his eyebrows in work, so he asked me to write the arrangements. It was to be recorded in Paris with the famous French vocal group, plus Bud Powell on piano, Pierre Michelot (bass), Kenny Clarke (drums), and Diz, of course. Mimi Perrin, musical director of the Double Six, was off on vacation in Italy. And since I had several concerts to play with trios (pick-up rhythm sections at jazz festivals along the Mediterranean), I decided to go from New York to Europe by sea.

I took the SS *United States*, and that first evening on the high seas I went into the bar. To my surprise (and pleasure), Miles Davis was there— and was going to play in some of the same festivals with his group. A journey by sea seemed a good way to prepare ourselves for the hectic schedules ahead, so we took advantage of this coincidence to sit down and have drinks together, gazing at the horizon, in which we were barely able to distinguish the timeless waters from infinite sky. Miles, perhaps unconsciously sensing the meaning of a space-time continuum, said, "I come from Diz (Gillespie), and Diz comes from Roy (Eldridge), and Roy comes from Louis (Armstrong)." I couldn't help but think about the genealogical tree of music history: Arnold Schoenberg influenced by Richard Wagner, who expanded the discoveries of Franz Liszt, Frederic Chopin, Johannes Brahms, and Hector Berlioz. And they followed Ludwig van Beethoven, who was influenced by Wolfgang Amadeus Mozart and Franz Joseph Haydn, and so on. Miles then further revealed that when younger he'd tried to play like Dizzy, but finally—wisely—came to the conclusion that it was impossible. So: he'd had to find his own, individual style, and of course it had proved very successful for him.

We decided to continue this very interesting conversation over dinner. However, in our first-class dining there was a "society" band. They were unobtrusive and of the kind that people could dance to in a nonswinging way. At the end of the set, the bandleader, who also played violin, came over to our table and said: "Mr. Davis and Mr. Schifrin, on behalf of the captain and the crew, we wish you a nice journey, and if you need anything else, please let us know." Miles looked at him and said, "How can you play this kind of shit? Don't you realize we are in 1963?" "Oh, but Mr. Davis," said the leader, "We can also play jazz." To which Miles retorted again, "Shit!" Needless to say, neither Miles nor I was invited to eat at the captain's table for the duration of that trip.

A little earlier, I had been on tour with Diz and Jazz at the Philharmonic, when we were sharing the bill with John Coltrane, Eric Dolphy, McCoy Tyner, and their group. John noticed that people were leaving during the first half of the concert while he was in mid-solo. On one of the plane trips between cities, he asked me why I thought this was happening. I didn't dare give him my *full* opinion: I'd too much respect for his tenor saxophone abilities for that. But since he'd asked me, my more cautious comment was "Perhaps you're playing My *Favorite Things* for forty-five minutes and people might get tired, or even a little bored—or maybe they still don't understand your innovations in Europe."[3]

John and I ended up developing a very nice friendship. He came to my house in New York and showed me the *Thesaurus of Scales and Melodic Patterns* by Nicolas Slonimsky. This book was his bible, and on one of the first pages is the chord progression of his own composition, *Giant Steps*.

I never did get to record with Miles. Or John.

Ray's Idea

During a *Jazz Meets the Symphony* concert in Los Angeles featuring James Moody, Jon Faddis, Ray Brown, Grady Tate, and the Glendale Orchestra, the famous bassist's music stand fell to the floor during the "Donna Lee" section of my "Charlie Parker: The Firebird" medley, which I was conducting from the podium. Ray started to talk to me, and I was bewildered: no musician, especially him, ever talks during a live performance. He kept on talking—but in the middle of the intense sounds of the group, the orchestra, not to mention the fact that there was a gigantic monitor loudspeaker between us, I was unable to understand what he was trying to stay. As a natural reaction, I checked my slacks, believing that Ray was trying to tell me that my fly was open, which was the only reason for his behavior that I could think of. His mouth kept moving and I looked at my fly again, but everything was in order.

Finally, the concert was over, and I found Ray Brown furiously complaining to my wife, "I kept asking Lalo what bar number we were on since my music was on the floor, and the silly man kept looking at his fly."

Notes

1. Gene used to write for *Down Beat* magazine; he has also written biographies of Henry Mancini, Woody Herman, and Oscar himself. Besides that, he was a great lyricist. He collaborated with Antonio Carlos Jobim in writing the English lyrics of "Quiet Nights" and set words to Bill Evans's exquisite "Waltz for Debby."

2. This was after the session recounted in the Sweet Sass vignette.

3. Later, I heard that when he was with Miles's quintet and sextet, the leader had criticized him for playing solos that were too long. John came on with the same answer he'd given me, "It takes so long to get off the ground, and when I'm up there I don't know how to come back." Miles had responded, sharply: "Try taking the horn off of your mouth, then!"

PART IV

INTERLUDE

CHAPTER SIXTEEN

~

International Incidents #2—The Cuban Missile Crisis

New York, October 1962, one of the most terrifying moments in history. The United States discovered Soviet nuclear missiles in Cuba, and after it had denounced the Soviet Union in the United Nations, the U.S. Navy proceeded to blockade the island and declare an exclusion zone around it. The conflict was reaching dangerous proportions, and President Kennedy, through his emissaries, was further denouncing Chairman Khrushchev's intentions.

While all of this was going on, I was preparing an innocent recording for Verve Records: *Piano, Strings and Bossa Nova*. The session was supposed to take place on Monday, October 29. It was difficult for me to concentrate on writing the orchestrations. The television was bringing frightening news: the blockade was regarded as an act of war, the Soviet ships were transporting more missiles to Cuba, and if the U.S. Navy boarded them, anything could happen. The frantic diplomatic activities at the Security Council seemed to be futile, and the specter of nuclear war was growing by the hour.

On Saturday the 27th, I went to have dinner at a club, the Blue Angel, in Manhattan, invited by the owner, a society lady connected to political and diplomatic circles. Like everybody else, I was praying for peace, and my anxiety to know if a solution to the crisis could be found led me to accept promptly. The dinner started in an atmosphere of tension, continual rumors feeding our state of agitation. After midnight, the Ghana ambassador to the United Nations, who at the time happened to be a member of the Security Council, arrived at the club and joined our table. He was livid, and despite his African origins, the color of his skin was frightfully pale. He said, "If by tomorrow we do not find a solution in which both parties can walk away without losing face, we may as well forget everything. There will be no more New York City." I said that I had a ticket to return to Argentina, which I had purchased the day before.[1] The ambassador looked at me and said, "If both superpowers exchange their nuclear arsenal, in the first two hours 300,000 people will be dead in both countries, and in three months there will not even be a plant alive on the whole planet." I responded nervously, "It is not the radiation that frightens me. I have a horror of blasts." Nobody laughed, but then it wasn't a joke.

The following day, Sunday the 28th, our prayers were answered, and the Soviet ships were returning to their ports of origin. Kennedy and Khrushchev made a deal, and the confrontation was avoided. On Monday, October 29, at 2:00 p.m., the downbeat went down on *Piano, Strings and Bossa Nova*. I canceled my return ticket to Buenos Aires, and life went on as if nothing had happened. That was my autumn in New York, where Dr. Strangelove met Antonio Carlos Jobim.

Note

1. A decision that was, obviously, based on self-preservation; I even forgot to cancel the recording sessions.

CHAPTER SEVENTEEN

~

Resonances

Tucuman, Argentina

It is possible that the keyboard becomes the mirror of time. In 1986, my wife, Donna, and I traveled to Buenos Aires, where I was engaged to conduct a tour with the National Symphony Orchestra of Argentina. One of the venues was the city of Tucuman, in the northwest. The native population of that part of the country used to be the vassals of the Incan Empire. In 1816, delegates from all the provinces declared Argentinean independence from Spain in that city. The House of Independence is in all the engravings and pictures in the history books, and its image is part of the collective memory of all Argentineans.

Since I had never been to Tucuman, Donna and I went to visit the House of Independence, which had become a museum. There was a warm feeling inside. The same philosophers who had inspired both the French Revolution and the framers of the U.S. Constitution influenced the delegates who participated in the historical assembly of 1816. Their Republican and Democratic ideas were the point of departure for a nation that, in spite of the future distortions of warlords, greedy politicians, and corrupt rulers, still survives and whose people have hopes for a better future. Inside the House Museum, I felt the link to my home country, and I could not hide my emotions. There were flags, swords, and the solemn book of the Act of Independence with all the signatures, and paintings and busts of the founding fathers of the United Provinces of the River Plate.

Donna and I were contemplating this solemn collection of memorabilia in silence when we suddenly noticed the piano, which turned out to be the very instrument on which the national anthem was played for the first time in Buenos Aires in 1813. The museum guards were observing us, and perceiving my curiosity about the piano—I was particularly interested in what its sound might be—asked me if I wanted to play it. After trying a few chords and arpeggios, I was pleasantly surprised to find that it was in perfect condition; I learned that the governor of the Tucuman Province at the time had taken care of the instrument and ensured that it was regularly tuned. One of the guards broke the intensity of the moment by requesting that I play "Mission: Impossible." I thought that doing so would be a sacrilege; instead my hands were impelled by a strange force to play the national anthem of Argentina.

In its original version, this is a mini-cantata with a long instrumental introduction and many stanzas of different shapes divided by difficult orchestral interludes, which lead to the last refrains and a triumphal coda. Blas Parera, who was very much influenced by Haydn, wrote the music. This is the version that I sang during my school years on national holidays, which were not too frequent. Obviously, I knew the work, but I had never played it on the piano: in retrospect it occurs to me that I could have committed an equal sacrilege by inflicting unforgivable mistakes. But my fingers flew over the keys, and the spirit of the anthem was well conveyed.

When we left through the gardens, the night embraced us with the perfume from the subtropical flowers. The second movement of my piano suite *Resonances* is a nocturne inspired by those wonderful memories.

Salzburg, Austria

In the late 1990s, I appeared at the Salzburg Music Festival to perform one of my *Jazz Meets the Symphony* programs. On the day of the concert, the festival's organizers took me to the home where Wolfgang Amadeus Mozart was born and spent his childhood; some members of the Mozarteum and other personalities were there as well.

I don't know how to describe my feelings. The furniture, the first violin and keyboards that the genius had played, and manuscripts of his earlier compositions transported me in time. I didn't dare say a word: any comment would have been trite and superfluous. Then I was asked if I wanted to try one of the keyboards. But this experience was different from the previous ones. How could I dare to touch those keys? There was a sense of purity (the same one that Mozart's music projects) that I did not want to violate. However, they kept insisting, so I sat and played a movement of one of his sonatas. Yet I was so careful about the fingering, the technical aspects, and above all not wanting to make a fool of myself through the transparency of the composition, that I felt curiously detached. I tried to save the day by trying to imitate Friedrich Gulda's phrasing and interpretation of the same work. The final chords were followed by cordial applause. The keyboard was not only a mirror of time; I had to face myself in it.

Since Mozart did not write the cadenzas of his piano concertos (they were improvised as they are in jazz), I suddenly ventured the cadenza that Beethoven wrote for Wolfgang Amadeus's first movement of the Piano Concerto No. 20, in C Minor. I love what Beethoven did with it, and I attacked it with all my concentration. Slowly I forgot the notes, and my hands were taking me in a different direction without losing the essence of Mozart's style. My improvisation explored all the motifs and themes of the first movement. My fingers were flying, and this time the emotion was felt all around me. I have no explanation for it. It would be presumptuous to pretend I was "possessed" by Mozart's spirit; I was merely playing a good improvisation in his musical idiom.

Perhaps it was another coincidence. Perhaps during my younger years, while studying his works, I "absorbed" his idiosyncrasies. Or maybe my improvisational experience led me to achieve a satisfying musical moment. There are some scientists whose theories propose that energy may remain in an object for a long time; I cannot usefully comment on that, but if it's true, I would give anything to play on Oscar Peterson's Bosendorfer!

Another rather less elevating but extremely funny incident occurred while I was in Salzburg at that time. In 1993, when working in London on the post-production of *More Jazz Meets the Symphony*, I received an urgent call from my European booking agent that the organizers of the Salzburg Music Festival wanted me to attend a press conference prior to the event. There was a lot of curiosity among television stations, journals, magazines, and newspapers about what *Jazz Meets the Symphony* was supposed to be. I had been hired to perform it at the festival two weeks later, and my participation at the press conference would help to promote my appearance at the festival in which Jon Faddis, James Morrison, Phil Woods, and the State Radio Orchestra from Munich, Germany, were booked.

After a whole evening at the CTS Studios in Wembley, Donna and I ran to the airport and arrived in Salzburg completely exhausted. Donna went to sleep at the hotel that had been provided to us, and I was taken immediately to the press conference. The promoter invited Donna, my agent, and me to a luncheon afterward. I was bombarded with questions that, despite my fatigue,

I answered the best I could. After all, my inner conviction about the validity of the endeavor gave me the strength to fence with the journalists and critics of the electronic and printed press.

Finally, around noontime, there were no more questions, and the television cameramen started to withdraw their equipment and, one by one, the participants started to wrap up. I was relieved and especially looking forward to the luncheon because, on top of everything else, I had not had breakfast on the airplane from London. But as I made ready to join my companions in the car, all of a sudden a young lady from the back of the conference room asked me, "Why did you write 'Mission: Impossible' in 5-4 rhythm?" I was speechless. How was I going to answer such a question since I composed it by instinct? Perhaps because I am a jazz musician, I improvised immediately the following answer:

"During the 1940s, the U.S. Armed Forces were conducting nuclear experiments in the New Mexico desert. The Manhattan Project's goal was to build the atomic bomb. During those experiments, the radiation contaminated the soil, and new babies were being born with five legs. When those unfortunate mutants were of the age to go dance in discotheques and clubs, they realized that all the music around is designed for people to dance to with two legs, so I wrote "Mission: Impossible" for them. After all, my endeavor was nothing new since toward the end of the nineteenth century there were sightings of flying saucers that descended in central Europe, and they were flown by aliens who had three legs. This fact influenced Johann Strauss and Franz Lehar to compose right here in Austria the waltz, which is in 3-4."

The young lady was writing furiously, noting my observations in great detail. I thought that she would get the joke, but, unfortunately, a few weeks later when I was back in Los Angeles, Burkhard Hopper (my agent) called me and said, "What are you trying to do? Did you know that this young journalist is the leading classical music critic in Vienna, and she writes for the city's most important classical musical publication?" Oblivious to my sense of humor, she had taken me literally, and my comments had been published as entirely serious analysis!

~

CHAPTER EIGHTEEN

International Incidents #3—*The Fourth Protocol* Redux

The Fourth Protocol was a British production, and the scoring sessions were supposed to take place in London. However, at the time, the British musicians were on strike, so the recording was moved to Paris.

While I was completing the music in Los Angeles, the Chernobyl nuclear disaster took place in the former Soviet Union. An acquaintance of mine (a fan who has been following my career) paid me a visit. A devoted music lover, he also happens to belong to one of the U.S. security agencies; he had, I believe, some kind of involvement in Dizzy's State Department tour.[1] He asked what I was doing. "I am going to Paris to work on a film score" was my response.

"No, you are not," he said. "The radiation has contaminated the whole European continent and beyond. There is radiation in Scotland," he added.

I showed him a copy of the weekly *Le Monde*, which claimed that France was safe.

"Do you think that the nuclear cloud believes in borders between countries?" he asked.

I had a contract to fulfill, and I could not breach my obligation. When he saw that I was determined and that nothing would deter my firm decision to fly to Europe, he said, "Okay, I will help you, but it has to be a secret, a total secret. Not even our foreign personnel is aware of what I am going to tell you: only our ambassadors know how to proceed in these circumstances. We don't want to create a panic."

So he gave me the following instructions: "You cannot drink any water, not even if it is bottled, only red wine that is older than the Chernobyl accident.[2] Also, no milk, or any dairy products, no meat, nor any poultry or vegetables. No bread, no desserts, no pasta, no fish from lakes or rivers. Only fish from the Mediterranean and canned food."

Finally he added, "Somebody is going to have to bring you a package with a special toothpaste, soap, and shampoo. Every time you come in from the street you must take a shower using the shampoo and soap." Then he departed, leaving me quite concerned.

The next day, the package arrived. Donna helped me to pack instant coffee and bottled water from here. She baked me special bread and put a lot of mozzarella cheese in the suitcases. Since I was staying at the Hotel Plaza Athenee, there was a refrigerator in the room where I could conveniently keep the food. As I arrived at the Paris airport, I walked through the "nothing to declare" line: if the customs officials had only known I was smuggling Evian water into France! Once at the hotel, I took the special shower and went to get a small electric kettle. Back in my room I took another shower with all the implements and went to sleep.

The next day, not being able to have delicious French croissants, I prepared my breakfast: instant coffee, Donna's bread, and mozzarella cheese. I was supposed to have lunch with the producer, Timothy Burrell, and the musician's contractor (who also owned the recording studio), Jean-Claude Dubois. They were waiting for me in a good restaurant near the Trocadero. The waiter brought me the menu, and I said I wasn't hungry, no salad or soup. "Do you have any canned food, like hearts of palms or sardines?"

"No, monsieur, everything in this restaurant is fresh," he said proudly.

I ended up having "loup de mer" and an old Bordeaux (no vegetables). My table companions were puzzled and thought I was eccentric, but the fish and wine were quite good. When I returned to the hotel I took another "shower." This routine continued for seven days and nights. It was difficult, especially because in France every meal is a ritual; during the sessions I was taking my own sandwiches to the studio and disappeared while the director, producer, and musicians were invading the many restaurants at the Palais des Congrès at lunchtime.

During that week in Paris, the French newspapers started to report the presence of radiation in Alsace, Nice, and other regions. There were even pictures of official scientists with Geiger counters in the supermarkets. And when I got back to Los Angeles, somebody sent by my music fan and security adviser came to my house to pick up my clothing and shoes in order to decontaminate them.

The irony is that *The Fourth Protocol* is about the plan by some members of the KGB to send an agent to England with a nuclear device. This time, life was far ahead of art!

Notes

1. I never asked him questions about his activities. We do not even talk about politics.
2. That was easy in France!

CHAPTER NINETEEN

~

International Incidents #4—Sofia

In 1991 I was commissioned by the Steinway Foundation in New York to write a piano concerto to celebrate the 500th anniversary of Christopher Columbus's first voyage to the new continent. It was my *Piano Concerto No. 2*, "The Americas," which was premiered by the National Symphony Orchestra at the Kennedy Center for the Performing Arts in Washington, DC, in the spring of 1992. Mstislav Rostropovich was the conductor, and a Brazilian pianist who resides in London, Cristina Ortiz, was the soloist.

The performance was well received. A gentleman from the United States Information Agency approached me right after the concert, and we decided to meet at the bar at the Watergate Hotel, where my wife and I were staying. He proposed organizing a European premiere in Sofia, Bulgaria, toward the year's end; the soloist was going to be Jenny Zacharieva, a Bulgarian pianist, and I was to conduct the Sofia Symphony Orchestra. Since I had never been in Eastern Europe before, and considering that it would present my new work under the best of conditions—by this time the old Soviet Empire was disintegrating—I naturally accepted.

Upon our arrival in the Bulgarian capital, we were welcomed by the representative of the orchestra, Jenny Zacharieva, and by members of the United States Information Agency. My wife and I were accompanied to the best hotel in Sofia, and that evening the U.S. ambassador and his wife invited us to a dinner at their residence. The following days, coming and going to rehearsals, I realized that many members of the CIA or other American agencies were staying at the hotel. In the elevator, they were talking openly about assignments in Latvia, Estonia, Georgia, and other republics of the former Soviet Union. And I was always accompanied (perhaps protected?) by these gentlemen. My wife and I decided to call them simply "CIA" without really knowing if they were really spies. We did not have any evidence of it, but it was good shorthand since we didn't know their names or what their function was.

One day, one of them asked me if after a rehearsal I would be willing to give a lecture to the composition students at the Music Academy. I could not refuse, and I was driven to a forbidding building, severe but with the charm of old Europe (providing that it was not used as an interrogation center during the Communist era). I was taken to the dean's office and shared cups of Turkish coffee with the faculty and the CIA, chatting informally. They were all smiling, in spite of the fact that the coffee was extremely bitter. Finally, it was time to go to the auditorium. I had thought that a few students of composition would attend, but the place was packed. There were more than two thousand young people who greeted me with an ovation! So far, so good.

The dean, the faculty, and the CIA sat in the first row. On stage with a microphone and a piano, my initial instincts were to talk about generalities and tell anecdotes or have them analyze my piano concerto, which was the reason for my visit to their country. But since I thought that something more was expected of me (perhaps a revelation) and wanted to stimulate my young audience with challenging thoughts, I proceeded to give a dissertation on the latest achievements and discoveries in contemporary music. After all, in nearby Poland a great movement of new music had been taking place since the 1970s.

As I was talking, I felt that the students were becoming uncomfortable. Their faces revealed nothing but blank, neutral expressions. Slowly, murmurs of discontent began to grow into chants of protest. I didn't understand what was happening. The dean, the faculty, and the CIA were expressionless. For a second I thought that they didn't understand English and that we would need an interpreter. Finally, I asked if they understood what I was saying, for I was discussing highly technical matters. Their angry answers were, "No, no, they don't teach us anything in this school! They advise us to study the old scores of the masters without any guidance or methodology."

I looked at the dean, the faculty, and the CIA: they were clearly getting restless, and I felt that I was going to be responsible for an international incident! All of a sudden, I asked the most vociferous protester if he was a composer. He said, "Yes!" "Okay, come to the piano and play one of your compositions so we can talk about it." And he did. Gradually, the audience became so engrossed that they began to calm down. I continued with this procedure with several students, and finally they forgot the reason for their anger. The dean, the faculty, and the CIA were smiling now.

The whole thing finished with another standing ovation. I could not understand the reason for it, because my careful comments and objective short analysis of their compositions did not merit such a demonstration. Nevertheless, when at the end, we went back to the dean's office with the faculty and the CIA, they all thanked me effusively as if nothing had happened.

The European premiere of my concerto "The Americas" was very successful, but the standing ovation at Sofia Hall was a few decibels lower than the one at the Music Academy. What a pity that Vernon Duke did not write a song "Wintertime in Bulgaria."

~

CHAPTER TWENTY

A Vignette Miscellany

Groucho Marx

In 1974, Donna and I decided to go to Europe for two weeks. During the first week I had to record my score for the film *The Four Musketeers*. The following week we were going to take a vacation in Paris. Prior to our trip, we asked my mother-in-law, Susie Cockrell, to come from Oklahoma to take care of little Ryan, who was one year old, and to supervise the household. We have quite a large home, and it needs a staff to take care of the garden, the swimming pool, and the cleaning, cooking, and other chores. Donna made sure that all electrical and other technical appliances would be in order so Susie would only have to concentrate on the baby, and her responsibilities would be greatly simplified. We specifically asked her not to open the door to anyone.

Away we went on our journey, which went very smoothly. I completed my film score in London and enjoyed working with the director, Richard Lester. In Paris we had a really good time visiting museums, shopping, and enjoying good food, sometimes in the company of friends.

Upon our return to Beverly Hills, Susie told us, "Guess who came to visit the house? Groucho Marx, but I did not let him in as you asked me not to let anyone in!"

Groucho Marx used to own the house and lived in it for many years. I had no idea! I bought the house through real estate agents from Ralph Edwards, who was a TV personality. He had acquired it from Groucho. So I tried to get in touch with him, but his telephone number was unlisted. I asked several friends and my agent to help me, to no avail.

But one day, Groucho came back. He was on a nostalgia trip and wanted to reminisce and travel back in time to his former fiefdom. He showed us the rooms where Harpo used to practice his harp and Chico worked on the piano. He told us that when he was having large dinner parties, he used the family room in which he converted the pool table into a big dining table. We were fascinated. He told us that Barbara Stanwyck used to live in the house next door and across the street, Jose Iturbi and Doris Day. And he also told us that he now lived not too far from us. We invited him to dinner the following week, and he showed up with piano sheet music from his repertoire. He loved to sing for our guests, and I accompanied him at the keyboard. Obviously he enjoyed being the center of attention, and we got along very well.

One evening, he invited us to his house, and several of his friends, including the writer Sidney Sheldon, were present. After the dinner, Groucho proceeded to tell us the origins of the Marx Brothers' success. Very early in their careers, they were Vaudeville singers in New York City. Their first tour took them to Texas; one of the stops was in the middle of the countryside, where an improvised theater was built. The public (mostly farmers) came on their customary mode of transport, on horseback, tying the horses in the corral next to the "stage," facing which were simple wooden benches. There were several acts before it was the Marx Brothers' turn; there were five of them at the time, and they began to sing. At that precise moment, the corral gate was accidentally opened, and the horses escaped. Panic spread through the audience, with everyone running to recapture his ride.

The Marx Brothers kept singing but gradually started to make fun of the absurd events. By the time the public returned, after recovering their horses, the performers had gone wild and were improvising witty jokes about the whole thing. They got big laughs and applause, and this proved the turning point in their careers—the moment in which they realized that they would have more success as comedians than singers.

By the time Groucho finished telling the story, everyone in his living room was enthralled. I may add that, although the aging process was evident, he was still a great master of the narrative arts. As Donna and I were leaving, I thought that his story was not only a colorful vignette of "Americana" but also a very important step in the history of show business. So I said to him, "Thank you so much for the invitation. I had one of the most memorable evenings ever." Loyal to his incomparable sense of humor, he cut me off with "You are very easily amused!"

We kept seeing each other off and on, though my constant travels and his deteriorating health made such encounters very difficult. However, the last time we were together he gave me his autobiography, *Groucho and Me*. The first lines are almost as memorable as those of Cervantes in *Don Quixote*.

"I was born in New York City because during such an important event I wanted to be very close to my mother."

Recently we saw a film of Groucho Marx walking through the front door of the house. From the outside it looks the same, although many renovations have been carried out since 1929, and I am sure that Groucho's spirit is around, playing his practical jokes and helping to reinforce the good humor of our family.

Audition

Zubin Mehta, who happens to be the music director of the Munich Opera, introduced me to a bass singer who was working with him on Wagner's *Ring Cycle*. The gentleman, whose name I do not remember, said very loudly, in the middle of the Bayerischer Hof Hotel's lobby, "Very nice meeting you" in an extremely deep voice. Zubin's comment to me was "You see, bass singers audition even when they are talking!"

Barbra Streisand

In *The Eagle Has Landed* there is a subplot, a love affair between Donald Sutherland and the British young lady who helps him in the plot to assassinate Winston Churchill. I had written and scored a love theme for those scenes, which were deleted in the final version because the film was far too long. However, I liked the theme so much that I recorded it in New York for Creed Taylor as an instrumental entitled "Eagles in Love."

Shortly after the record was released, Barbra Streisand called me in Los Angeles and said, "I like that melody; does it have any lyrics? I am planning to record an album in which the concept is around water, tears, rain and the like, and I would very much like to include your song."

I told her that it did not have lyrics and I could contact her favorite lyricists, Alan and Marilyn Bergman, suggesting that she explain her concept to them. Although they were in New York working on a musical, after a few days they came up with the words for the song "On Rainy Afternoons," which was going to be included on Barbra's upcoming album, *Wet*. She phoned me again and said, "I like the lyrics, and I want you to write the arrangement." I had heard horror stories from my colleagues about how difficult she was; I once saw a very prominent composer-arranger emerge from the recording studio in which he was working with her looking totally devastated.

So I told her, "You have so many arrangers who are so used to your style, why don't you hire one of them?"

"No," she said, "I like the orchestration you did in the instrumental version, and I would like it to be the same—in my key, of course!"

We made an appointment to fix it in her key. I sat at the piano, and while enjoying her marvelous voice, I started to change the harmonies in Monkish fashion.[1] Barbra interrupted my playing and said, "What happened, are you getting tired of your own composition? Don't tamper with success." I had forgotten that she comes from the Broadway tradition where everything is predetermined and rehearsed until it becomes what they call "routine." But I had to give her the benefit of the doubt. After all, she was Barbra Streisand, she had worked with Leonard Bernstein, and her point was entirely valid. I had accepted the assignment to write the same orchestration in her key, and I should keep my word to the letter. This was *not* jazz.

Anyway, she told me to be at Capitol Records at exactly 12:00 midnight a week later. I went a little early and felt as if I were at the dentist. ("Next case!") One arranger after another was taking turns conducting the orchestra. At 12:00 midnight it was time for me to get to the podium. She is so great that we completed the recording in one take. I was out of the studio at 12:05 a.m.

Ironically, that was the same studio where Stan Getz had said, "No, man, this is jazz, and you had your chance. . . ." Perhaps the Broadway tradition of the "routines" helps to freeze time and postpone the aging process; it may even be a way to seek immortality!

The Statue (Pavarotti)

I attended a business meeting in Luciano Pavarotti's apartment in New York along with his conductor, to prepare an upcoming performance with the Vienna Opera. All of a sudden, a beautiful young lady appeared accompanied by a young man. "I was late for the Luciano Pavarotti International Competition, and you told me to come today." Pavarotti said, "Did you bring the music?" "No," said the young lady. Pointing at the young man, Pavarotti said, "Is he your accompanist?" "No, he's my boyfriend."

So, Pavarotti got the music she was supposed to sing, and the conductor and I took turns at the piano. She proceeded to sing, or rather, try to: her voice was far from nice, her intonation was nonexistent, her lack of control quite pitiful, and her phrasing totally disjointed.

Headshot of Lalo Schifrin. Lalo Schifrin at 22 years of age,
Paris, France. *Schifrin personal collection.*

Lalo Schifrin at piano. Lalo Schifrin, age 26, Buenos Aires, Argentina. *Schifrin personal collection.*

Performance photo of *Cantos Aztecas.* Lalo Schifrin conducting. Soloists (left to right): Martha Felix, Conchita Julian, Placido Domingo, Nikita Storojev. Teotihuacan, Mexico, October 1998. *Photo property of Aleph Records.*

Rehearsal for *Latin Jazz Suite* recording. (Left to right) David Sanchez, Jon Faddis, Lalo Schifrin. Cologne, Germany, 1999. *Photo property of Aleph Records.*

Recording session of *More Jazz Meets the Symphony*. (Left to right) James Morrison, Paquito D'Rivera, Jon Faddis, Grady Tate, Ray Brown, Lalo Schifrin (seated at piano). CTS Studios, London, England, December 1993. *Photographer: Catherine Ashmore. Photo property of Aleph Records.*

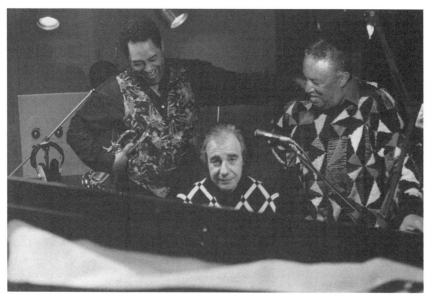

Recording of *Firebird*. (Left to right) Jon Faddis, Lalo Schifrin, Ray Brown. CTS Studios, London, England, 1995. *Photographer: Karl Grant. Photo property of Aleph Records.*

Rehearsal for *Latin Jazz Suite*. (Left to right) Lalo Schifrin, David Sanchez, Jon Faddis. Los Angeles, CA, 2001. *Photographer: Tony Gieske.*

Lalo and Donna Schifrin. 1999. *Schifrin personal collection.*

Three-quarter figure shot of Lalo Schifrin. September 2000. *Photographer: Joel Lipton.*

Cannes Film Festival jury members. (Left to right) Lalo Schifrin, Clint Eastwood, Cather-ine Deneuve. Cannes, France, May 1994. *Schifrin personal collection.*

Post-concert celebrating Dizzy Gillespie's seventieth birthday. (Left to right) James Moody, Dizzy Gillespie, Lalo Schifrin. Wolftrap, VA, June 1987. *Schifrin personal collection.*

Post-concert Lalo Schifrin and Dizzy Gillespie. 1984 Olympic Games. Los Angeles, CA. *Photographer: Joseph Tanur. Schifrin personal collection.*

Lalo Schifrin's fiftieth birthday celebration. (Left to right) Lalo Schifrin, Don Siegel, Clint Eastwood. Schifrin home, Beverly Hills, CA, June 1982. *Schifrin personal collection.*

Recording session for Jose Carreras. CTS Studios, London, England, March 1992. *Schifrin personal collection.*

Lalo Schifrin and Martin Landau. Schifrin home, Beverly Hills, CA, 1990.
Schifrin personal collection.

Cantos Aztecas performance. Lalo Schifrin conducting. Soloist: Placido Domingo. Teotihuacan, Mexico, October 1998. *Photo property of Aleph Records.*

Lalo Schifrin and Chucho Valdez. Catalina Bar and Grill, Los Angeles, CA, 2000. *Photographer: Bonnie Perkinson.*

Lalo Schifrin and Francis Ford Coppola at anniversary screening of *THX 1138*. Guggen-heim Museum, New York City, September 2004. *Photographer: Dave Alloca. Photo property of Warner Home Video.*

Post-performance of world premiere of Schifrin's Piano Concerto No. 2. (Left to right) Lalo Schifrin, Mistlav Rostropovich, Christina Ortiz. Kennedy Center, Washington, DC, 1992. *Schifrin personal collection.*

Rehearsal for *Christmas in Vienna*. (Left to right) Lalo Schifrin, Jose Carreras, Diana Ross, Placido Domingo. Vienna, Austria, 1992. *Schifrin personal collection.*

Lalo Schifrin and Herbie Hancock. Los Angeles, CA, 2000. *Schifrin personal collection.*

Lalo Schifrin with Dizzy Gillespie. Los Angeles, CA, February 1977. *Photographer: Phil Stern.*

Lalo Schifrin and Ella Fitzgerald at concert rehearsal. Hollywood Bowl, Hollywood, CA, 1995. *Photographer: Joseph Tanur. Schifrin personal collection.*

Lalo Schifrin and George Lucas. Guggenheim Museum, New York City, September 2004. *Photographer: Dave Alloca. Photo property of Warner Home Video.*

Lalo Schifrin and Paul Newman on location for *Cool Hand Luke*. Stockton, CA, 1967. *Schifrin personal collection.*

Quincy Jones and Lalo Schifrin. Los Angeles, CA, 2001. *Schifrin personal collection.*

Toots Thielemans and Lalo Schifrin. Vibrato Jazz Club, Los Angeles, CA, 2005. *Schifrin personal collection.*

Zubin Mehta and Lalo Schifrin at party for Israeli Philharmonic Orchestra. Los Angeles, CA, 1991. *Schifrin personal collection.*

Jazz Meets the Symphony recording. (Left to right) Lalo Schifrin, James Morrison, Paquito D'Rivera, Grady Tate, Jon Faddis, Ray Brown. CTS Studios, London, England, 1992. *Property of Aleph Records.*

Lalo Schifrin with The Three Tenors on eve of finals of soccer World Cup. (Left to right) Jose Carreras, Placido Domingo, Luciano Pavarotti, Lalo Schifrin. Paris, France, 1994. *Photo property of Clarin Newspaper.*

MISSION IMPOSSIBLE

LALO SCHIFRIN

Jay Leno Show

LALO SCHIFRIN, BMI

"Mission: Impossible." *Music by Lalo Schifrin, published by Famous Music.*

Mission: Impossible original cast and producers at soundtrack recording party. (Left to right) Bruce Geller, Barbara Bain, Martin Landau, Bill Stinson, Peter Graves, Lalo Schifrin, Peter Lupus, Gregg Morris, Paramount records executive. Hollywood, CA, 1967. *Photo property of Jeanette Geller.*

After several different tries with different arias, Luciano finally stopped her and asked her to sit in front of him by his desk. This piece of furniture was very big, and among other objects on it was a large equestrian statue.

"Have you been studying a long time?" asked Pavarotti.

"Oh, yes, many years," said the young lady.

"Do you have a teacher?"

"Yes, I take lessons twice a week."

"Are the lessons expensive?"

"Yes, quite!"

"So you have spent a lot of money on your vocal education?"

"Oh, yes."

Then Pavarotti showed her the equestrian statue on top of his desk. "Do you see this statue, how beautiful it is? Please observe the perfect features of the horse, his fine legs, the sense of motion, the precision with which the horseman has been sculpted, how graceful he looks to the last detail."

"Yes, I can see."

"Now, observe the marble out of which the work of art has been sculpted. This marble is quite special: please observe the surface, its perfect texture."

"Yes, an effect I can see."

"You see? The sculptor had something to work with. But you don't have the marble."

The young lady was silent.

Collateral Damage

During a performance by Jose Carreras of the last tragic act of Puccini's *Tosca*, in which he has to be executed by Scarpia's guards, a grave error took place on stage. As one of the most beautiful melodies in the history of opera came to an end as a sort of final farewell to Tosca, the extras that were portraying the guards shot Tosca instead of Caravadossi (Carreras). She was on the other side of the stage. So Carreras, who according to the libretto had to die (otherwise the opera would not be able to end), fell to the floor, pretending to have a heart attack. Tosca kept singing. . . .

Self-Defense

Pierre Boulez is one of the greatest musicians of our time. As a composer, he not only achieved a synthesis of Anton Webern and Olivier Messiaen's dissimilar concepts in the avant-garde, he expanded them to the point where he found his own musical vocabulary. As a conductor, he gained the respect of every musician who worked under his baton.

He has a phenomenal ear. When I was a student in Paris, he was rehearsing one of his own compositions. The vibraphonist had to play seventeen fast notes in one beat. Boulez stopped him and said, "The eleventh note is an A flat and not an A natural." The vibraphone player said, "Pardon, maitre."

On another occasion, a piccolo player was late for the rehearsal, so Boulez whistled his parts while conducting the other musicians. His reputation was such that when he became musical director of the New York Philharmonic, the members of the orchestra called him the French Correction.

One time I asked him with whom he had studied the baton technique. His answer was "Since nobody could conduct my music, I became a conductor in self-defense."

Recently, in Berne, Switzerland, he was arrested as a terrorist because in the security police's computers there were documented his manifestos from his youth: "Schoenberg is dead: we must burn all the Opera Houses!"[2]

The Little Bell: Armand Molinetti

During the summer of 1955, while I was studying in France, a jazz tour of various ensembles of all-star European musicians and fashion models was sponsored by the renowned high fashion companies of Paris. The concerts would start with different groups playing modern jazz, and during the intermission there would be a fashion show accompanied by a trio. The drummer, Armand Molinetti, was known as a practical joker, and on several occasions he pretended to have a heart attack during the fashion show.

During the tour, we traveled to the town of Quimper, a seaport in Normandy. After we checked into our hotel, Molinetti suggested a walk in the town's commercial district—to me and a young Belgian tenor who was born near where the Battle of Waterloo took place. He was about eighteen, and his baby face made him look even younger; Molinetti was about thirty-five. I did not accept because I was planning to practice the piano before dinner, so Molinetti left with Waterloo.[3]

One hour before the show, the promoter, models, and musicians were eating around a large table in the restaurant next to the theater. All of a sudden, Molinetti walked in and asked for an individual table and pretended he did not know us. A few minutes later, Waterloo did the same and sat at a table next to Molinetti's. We all knew that they were plotting something, but we didn't have any idea what.

Suddenly, it all starts.

Waterloo (forte): Sir, what are you staring at?

Molinetti: Pardon me?

Waterloo: Sir, I asked you what you are staring at. I don't like to eat while somebody is staring at my face!

The waiter comes to see what's happening.

Molinetti: I said, pardon me!

This kind of exchange continues, louder and louder; the maître d' tries, vainly, to quiet things down.

Waterloo (rising from his table and throwing the napkin to the floor): That's it! I said that it makes me very uncomfortable to be stared at in my face while I am eating!

Molinetti: I am sorry, but you remind me of someone.

Waterloo: I don't care who I remind you of! Just leave me alone!

Molinetti: No, you don't understand. My wife and I had a son that looked exactly like you. We lost him in the last war. He went to the front, and the only thing he took with him was a small family souvenir . . . a little bell.

Waterloo (becoming pale and bewildered): A little bell?

Molinetti: Yes, a little bell.

Waterloo (taking from his pocket a brass bell that they had bought at an antiques shop earlier in the afternoon): Papa!

Molinetti: My son!

They both kiss and hug each other in the middle of the restaurant to the obvious surprise of the customers and personnel.

Needless to say, at our table we had to exercise a great deal of restraint and control to avoid contagious laughter. I was chewing on my napkin with tears streaming down my face.

Hydrophobia

Igor Stravinsky told me that in the 1940s Sergei Rachmaninoff, who was a virtuoso pianist and also a composer (more conservative than Stravinsky), came to Los Angeles to perform at the Hollywood Bowl. They were both born in Russia, and despite their different aesthetic approach to music, they were friends. Stravinsky and his wife, Vera, invited the Rachmaninoffs for dinner in their home (which was close to my present residence). During the dinner, Rachmaninoff's wife asked the host, "Maestro, what is you daily work routine?" Stravinsky said, "I wake up early in the morning, I eat breakfast, then I take a shower. After the shower I go to my studio and I start to work." Rachmaninoff's wife said to her husband, "You see, he takes a shower!"

Retroactive Loyalties

During one of our vacations in Venice, Italy, my wife and I decided to visit the house where W.A. Mozart lived while he was working in that city.

On that day, we found the museum closed. I knocked at the big door, and there was no answer. In front there was a commemorative sign verifying that we were indeed at the right place. I kept knocking even louder. Finally, a lady opened a window on the second floor. I speak Italian quite fluently,[4] and I asked the lady at the window if Donna and I could visit the museum. She said that it would be closed during the weekend. "If you come on Monday, Mozart will be here and you can talk to him." (She was entirely serious.) Unfortunately, we had to leave on Sunday. I regret the fact that I never got to ask Amadeus if Salieri was such a bad guy. Also, I wanted to know his opinion about the cadenzas to his *Piano Concerto No. 20* written by Beethoven and Brahms. Oh well, next time, perhaps, or maybe I'll request a meeting with his assistant in Salzburg. . . .

The first day we arrived in Rome, we decided to view the ruins of the Coliseum, the Forum, and the Palatinum. A German archeologist who was working on the layers beneath the ancient city was convinced that I was a history teacher because I asked him about Numa Pompilius and Tullius Hostilius, who were two of the first kings of Rome. So he made it possible for Donna and me to visit Livia's house in the Palatinum. A guard out of a Fellini film, with gold teeth, was in charge of the ancient mansion, and he showed us the bedroom, the dining room, and the original furniture. It was fascinating to be in the living quarters of the Emperor's wife and to get a sense of how the old Roman elite used to live and to get a feel for their everyday life.

I said to Donna, in front of the guard, "Livia was a nymphomaniac, and when her husband Augustus was away, commanding the Imperial conquests, she made love every night to a different legionnaire and then had him killed." The guard with the golden teeth became furious and said to me, "Those are lies and unfounded rumors. The Empress was the holiest woman in Rome!"

When we left, he closed the door and stayed in Livia's home. He probably was a little unbalanced from staying in that environment all the time and had grown fond of working for the ghost of what had once been his First Lady; time had stood still and he was proud of his job. After living in Hollywood for a while, and knowing how many rumors and innuendos are fabricated about movie stars, I thought that he was probably right and I should be working for a tabloid gossip magazine.

We then went to Vienna, where after the museums and Sigmund Freud's house, we attended a performance of *Othello* at the Opera. The old ladies were crying at the end of the last act. The following day we visited Haydn's home, which is a museum. This one was open, and I was not allowed to play the different keyboards on display. A tour guide showed us the living quarters of Joseph Haydn's servant, who was also his cook, his driver, and . . . his copyist!

Upon our return to Los Angeles, Donna dissuaded me from asking my music copyist to cook or drive for us. . . .

O Tempora! O Mores!

Some Notes on Critics

On a Saturday night, I asked Alicia de Larrocha, one of the greatest Spanish pianists of our time, if she had read the excellent reviews she got in the *Los Angeles Times* for a recital she played the previous Thursday.

She said, "I never read my reviews since an incident that happened to me in Tulsa, Oklahoma. It was announced that I would play the *Beethoven Concerto No. 1 for Piano and Orchestra*. However, right before that tour I decided to change the program and play *Mozart's No. 20*.

"When I arrived at the theater for my second concert, the musicians in the orchestra told me, 'It seems you play a great Beethoven.'

"'What do you mean?'

"The critic did not know about the program change, and either he did not attend the concert or he did not know the difference between *Mozart's No. 20* and the Beethoven 1st."

Therefore and thereafter, Alicia gave up on reading reviews.

My piano teacher in Argentina told me that the Russian composer Rimsky-Korsakov was disappointed because not only did none of his sons choose a musical career, but to make things worse, one of them went on to become a music critic.

Juan Carlos Paz, my composition teacher, was also a composer. His music was extremely avant-garde, and paraphrasing Dizzy, "not only difficult to understand but hard to listen to." Actually, he was a great composer, and it was the public's loss not to try and cooperate and reach the depths of his works.

Once the very orchestra of which my father was the concertmaster premiered in Buenos Aires one of Paz's works, *Labyrinth*. The reviews were devastating and even cruel. However, his comment about the hostile press was a quotation of an old Chinese proverb: "The one who stops during his journey every time a dog barks will never reach his destination."

On the other hand, Baudelaire said, "A critic is a dreamer whose spirit reaches towards the generalization and at the same time towards the study of details; better yet, towards the idea of a universal order."

Notes

1. Thelonious Monk had recorded an album, *Standards*, where he plays the melodies with great respect, but his innovation is in the way he transforms and creates new harmonies.

2. See chapter 3, Fugue.

3. I do not remember his real name, but everyone called him by this nickname.

4. In Argentina there is a large Italian colony. Even the Spanish accent prevalent in Buenos Aires sounds Italian. In Venice, people kept asking me what part of Italy I was from.

PART V

FILM

~

CHAPTER TWENTY-ONE

Composing for Film and TV

Routines and Processes

Sometimes a script is sent to me. However, this is not a sure indication of how the final movie is going to be. On some occasions, after I accept the assignment and my agent makes the deal regarding my participation, I must wait nine to twelve months for the casting, screenplay, and rewrites, the process of principal photography and editing, and I end up being very disappointed with the results. Nevertheless, since I have signed the contract, I must work the best way I can to make a musical contribution.

In any event, my specific involvement starts at the "spotting" session. After seeing the final movie, I sit with the director to decide the sequences and segments—"spots"—that need to be scored. This is a very important process. There are many ways to start and end a cue. The *Bullitt* "chase" is a perfect example. A music editor takes notes during the spotting session and breaks it down to hundredths of a second; I receive the notes by messenger, and then, in my studio, with the help of a computer book that gives me by frames and sprockets the detailed information to help me proceed, I synchronize the music exactly.

My work routine is built around a projected quota of how many minutes of music I need to write each day. Early in the morning I go to my gymnasium, where I use the treadmill and weights. [I used to do karate and other martial arts to the point that I became a black belt; before that I used to play tennis.] After exercising, I practice piano for one to two hours. After that I take a shower and eat lunch, and I look to start composing by 2:00 p.m. Most of the time, I close my studio at dinnertime, but on some occasions I have had to work late into the night, sometimes until 2:00 in the morning.

When composing, I have in my hands the music editor's notes and a video transfer (with time code) on the TV in front of me. First, I look for themes that can be transformed in function of the dramatic development of the movie. Sometimes secondary motifs are necessary. In *The Fourth Protocol*[1] there is a suspenseful scene in which Michael Caine is watching traffic-jammed cars on the road; inside one of them is Pierce Brosnan, who is the Russian villain. So I decided to go for a *passacaglia* technique borrowed from classical music—a bass line (piano, low strings, bass clarinet, bassoons) that has a menacing mood. Some sporadic drums play para-military figures in the open spaces, and string clusters are featured on top. Then woodwinds and muted trumpets are added, and trombones begin to join the intermittent bass theme, and the piece builds inexorably to the scene's climax.

Film music possibilities are infinite, as in any art form. For instance, in *Rollercoaster* (which stars George Segal, Henry Fonda, Richard Widmark, and Timothy Bottoms), I was confronted with a different kind of thriller in which an extortionist terrorizes amusement parks with highly dangerous explosives. My approach to the score was to create sounds based on the environments: calliope, merry-go-rounds, and children's rides contribute to establish an au-diovisual counterpoint—the innocent music almost indifferent to the horror on the screen. In addition, with the orchestra, especially the strings, I created a kind of relentless clock-like motif that conveys simultaneously the obses-sive mind of the villain and the ticking bomb that is about to explode.

However, in the Spanish film *Don Quixote* I used a different technique. When the wandering knight hallucinates, for example, the screen shows his point of view, like monstrous giants; my score is appropriately ominous, re-flecting his impressions. But when Sancho Panza sees that those objects are not giants but only real windmills, the music stops abruptly, and sound effects such as the breeze replace the music on the soundtrack. This device is used in every episode of that kind.

Yet another aspect that film composers must take into consideration is the so-called source music—that is, music coming from live music on the screen or juke boxes, radios, and so on. In *Telefon*, starring Charles Bronson, I had to score the music from a cartoon in a TV set during a scene in a hotel room. And in *Voyage of the Damned* I had to be present in Barcelona and London during the shooting so as to supervise live musicians "performing" on the screen.

The latter movie takes place during the Nazi regime (1938) and is about Jewish refugees leaving the port of Hamburg and arriving in Havana, Cuba.

There were German military bands, (some first-class, others less good), and Cuban musicians at the Havana harbor. After this first process, I had to write the dramatic underscore, waiting for the completion of principal photography and editing. Since not all the "source" music is recorded *in situ*, I combined the final symphonic score with some sessions dedicated to live bands, in which most of the time the extras on the screen play along with a pre-existing record.

A funny misunderstanding happened in this area. Stuart Rosenberg wanted a real German march from Hitler's era, but such marches are forbidden in postwar Germany. Nevertheless, somebody in London got a hold of one, entitled "Children of the Regiment"; I played it for Stuart at the piano, and he approved. After the main scoring sessions ended, I recorded the source music. When it came to "Children of the Regiment," after the first take Stuart called me to the recording booth. "It doesn't work," he said, "It is too happy, it sounds like circus music." My response was that he himself chose it and that it was in the style of German marches of that tragic period, but Stuart still objected. So at lunchtime I wrote my own march in a Wagnerian style, which I titled "The Housepainter March," subtitled "Hitler's Blues." Stuart approved it, and the final version remained in the movie.

Finally, the other way to do it is to write the music before shooting takes place, as I did in the Carlos Saura film *Tango*. The final process of my work in films, after the score (a single sheet showing the notation for each instrument) is completed, is to send it to the copyist, who extracts the parts for each one of the musicians.

It takes about six weeks to write the music for a movie. Then the scoring (i.e., recording) sessions take place in special studios that have sophisticated synchronization techniques. If the recording is made on twenty-four or forty-eight channels, a mix-down session is needed between composer and engineer in order to balance the different orchestral or electronic sounds.

Sixties Assignments

In 1967, one year after the debut of *Mission: Impossible*, Bruce Geller created a show called *Mannix*. Computers were emerging at this time, and Bruce's idea was about a detective who works with these instruments. The star of *Mannix* was Mike Connors, and the show was produced by Paramount.

At the same time Fox Studios, through a producer named Paul Monash, was creating another show called *Braddock* with a very similar premise. I was called from Fox to write the music for *Braddock*. I carefully tried to write two completely different scores, but the producers found out about my involvement with their respective competitors.[2] From my point of view it was great, because it is not easy to sell a pilot and develop it into a series. So I had nothing to lose. On the contrary, it was "heads I win, tails I win." Paul Monash asked me very nervously, "How does *Mannix* look?" Bruce Geller posed the same question about *Braddock*. In the end *Mannix* was bought and lasted seven years on the air.

Other shows for which I worked were *Medical Center, Starsky and Hutch, Petrocelli, T.H.E. Cat,* and *The Blue Light.* I also wrote the score for the first two-hour television movie, *See How They Run.* This television work was exhausting, but I paced myself by not writing all the episodes. [Other composers were rotating.] My advantage was that since they were using my themes, my credits and royalties were not affected; on the other hand, it was hard work, because I was doing my own orchestrations. All that said, it was satisfying to create distinctive themes for that popular medium; for example, the visual titles of *Medical Center* start with an ambulance (animation) coming from a distance toward the viewer. So with a synthesizer I imitated the sound of a siren, which becomes a melody.

Perhaps the function of music in TV themes is that, for example, the viewer is in the kitchen getting a soft drink, and the theme coming from the TV set lets him know that his favorite show is about to start.

The Exorcist

William Friedkin met me in Chicago in the early sixties, where I was performing with Diz. He was a young filmmaker and told me that he loved *Gillespiana*. On one of my free evenings, Friedkin invited me to have dinner at his place and to show me a documentary he had just completed. He also indicated his interest in my collaboration with him on scoring his film. After the meal was over, he showed me a powerful documentary about an African American prisoner on death row waiting for his execution. But Friedkin, through interviews and investigation, proved that this man was innocent or at least that there was reasonable doubt about his guilt. Finally, the documentary was so strong that the governor of Illinois gave a pardon to the unfortunate man, who happened to be at the wrong place at the wrong time when a crime was committed. As I was leaving Friedkin's place, he asked me if I would like to score his film; I responded with enthusiasm that it would be a great artistic challenge that I would gladly welcome.

Upon my return to the hotel, I saw police cars and a lot of commotion. I was not allowed to take the elevator to my floor. The concierge said to me,

"Something terrible has happened. Mr. Gillespie was the victim of an armed robbery." I was finally able to go to Dizzy's room, and he told me the story: two armed robbers broke into his room and took all the cash (the band's payroll for the previous week of the club where we'd appeared). Obviously it was an inside job. I had never seen Dizzy in such a state of terror, fear, and anger. He did not speak for two weeks and was in a very somber mood during that period until the emotional wound gradually began to heal. I am sure that his wife, Lorraine, was a great support, and we in the band tried to help him. But I'll never forget his eyes, which reflected that terror, fear, and anger.

Years later, when I was working in Hollywood, I ran into Friedkin again at Wolper Productions where I was working on *The Rise and Fall of the Third Reich* documentary. He was preparing a piece about police work in Los Angeles. I believe it was called *The Thin Blue Line*. It was not surprising to me that he would end up in Hollywood because he is really talented. He won a well-deserved Oscar for *The French Connection* and became one of the most promising young directors in the movie industry.

Around this time, rumors started to spread about a darker side to Friedkin's personality. Initially I ignored them: human nature sometimes cannot tolerate success, and tabloid newspapers and other sources of bad news try to level those who earn recognition and bring them down by other means. But I was to change my mind.

In 1973, Friedkin was working on *The Exorcist*, based on William Blatty's best-selling book of the same title. He called my agent and invited me to have a meeting in New York City. I noticed that he had changed. He did not look me in the eyes. His demeanor was a mixture of arrogance and levity, which I attributed to the big job he had to do, the sense of responsibility, and the normal insecurity that all artists go through during the creative process. Finally, he hired me for the job. I prepared myself by reading the book several times and also consulting members of the Catholic church; I even got a book about the music of the black masses in the Middle Ages. This was dangerous terrain, but I was spiritually so secure that I didn't think I was playing with fire.

When Friedkin finally showed me the film, I recognized his enormous talent as a director. *The Exorcist* is a very powerful movie, but also very disturbing, which is obviously what he wanted to achieve. Friedkin is a music aficionado, buys a lot of records, and in general has good taste. So when we talked specifically about the contribution the music would bring to the film, I suggested two string orchestras and special percussion (metal) instruments played with cellos and double bass bows, as they are easy extensions of the strings.

The next meeting took place at Warner Bros. Studios in Burbank, California—the always important session when the director and the composer decide the places where music is needed, and the nature of that music in each instance. The film editor and music editor usually attend this "spotting" session also. Because of the pressure of the deadline for a release date of the film, Friedkin asked me to do it as soon as possible on a Sunday morning.

However, when I showed up at the screening room with my music editor, I was shocked to find that he had invited a whole entourage of groupies, friends, and sycophants. It was impossible to concentrate and focus in the middle of whispers, nervous laughter, and all kinds of comments bouncing around the room. We finally succeeded in pinning down some decisions, but I found the director's attitude contemptible. I told him that if I had known that instead of a spotting session he was going to have a party, I would have stayed home with my family. As I realized later, he never forgave me for this.

He called me a few days afterward and asked me to write a six-minute piece for the "trailer" (coming attractions), with the intention to test the reaction of the audiences. So one week later we were at the recording studio with the musicians, the sound engineer, and the different assistants. The sound engineer told me that to record two string orchestras would only be possible for a stereo record, but at the time most of the movie theaters did not have the facilities to separate them. And it was more convenient for him to go the conventional way: first violins, second violins, violas, cellos, and double basses.

We went ahead on that basis. Friedkin showed real enthusiasm and told me many times how much he liked it. His reaction gave me the indication of the style that he was expecting from my contribution to the final movie. But things changed while I was working on the real process of creating the musical atmosphere for the film.

The trailer (coming attractions) had a mixed reaction from the public. The combination of frightening scenes with my scary music had almost a negative effect. The studio instructed Friedkin to tell me to tone down the score, which would have been very easy for me to do. However, William Friedkin failed to convey such important information. Later on I tried to attribute his lapse as the result of being so busy on the post-production details, the pressure of finishing the film, and suchlike. But to this day I still cannot believe that I was wrong: I had been set up. After the incident during the scoring session, I was told by two reliable sources, William Blatty, the author of the book and one of the producers on the film, and the film editor (who had been fired) that I was purposely set up. I couldn't quite see why this might be so, but by now I was hearing plenty of horror stories about what was going on—Friedkin's temper tantrums, dismissing friendly advice, terminating the services of his collaborators. At one point I started to think that being involved with such a project for about one year had affected his personality, almost as if he had been possessed by the malignant energies coming from the screen, the very images he had created. But I dismissed that thought. After all, Friedkin was a professional and there is in Hollywood a saying, "It is only a movie." However, the facts were going to prove me wrong.

The recording day arrived in October of 1973, close to Halloween day! After listening to a few music sequences, Friedkin walked out of the studio; shortly afterward I was informed that he wanted to see me in the office of the head of the Warner Bros. music department. He started to scream, foam was coming out of his mouth, "Where are the two string orchestras? This is not what we talked about! This music is not going to be in my film!" I was quiet and decided not to argue because he was out of control. There was no reasoning with him, and I knew that the whole scene could have ended in a physical confrontation. I did not want to spend the evening in jail, so I waited until he walked out. Larry Marks, who was the head of the music department, told me that Friedkin already had a group in mind—Tubular Bells—and the help of a composer, the late Jack Nitzsche. It was like a stab in the back. I drove home with my wife and felt depressed. But depression is anger turned inward. William Blatty came to my defense and made public declarations to the press, and the ex–film editor confirmed Blatty's comments about the setup. All Friedkin could respond with was that I had written a score with "Mexican maracas"!

Luckily, on the twenty-fifth anniversary of The Exorcist's release, the whole soundtrack was released, including my music. There were rumors that I had used my rejected score on The Amityville Horror, for which I was nominated for an Oscar. The Warner Bros. CD release disproves both assertions: there are not any Mexican maracas, and there is not one bar of music from The Amityville Horror.

From this disagreeable experience I also learned a valuable lesson: arrogant and contemptuous people must be carefully avoided. And above all, one must stay away from those who try to instill terror, fear, and anger. A few years ago I was invited by the organizers of the Glasgow Film Festival to attend a symposium, but I was warned that William Friedkin would be there and that they were going to talk about The Exorcist. I declined the invitation. No more Faustian pacts if I can avoid them.

The Politics of Film

In the book *From Caligari to Hitler* written by Siegfried Kracauer (the former conservator of the Museum of Modern Art in New York City), the author offers the theory that when a genre of movies or TV becomes popular, that this is due to its appeal to the collective unconscious and the public's consequent readiness to accept it. The producers, by trial and error, give the people what they are prepared to like.

During and after the Second World War, many films were made about Hitler and the Nazis: they were the obvious villains. After the war was over, a new conflict started, which we know as the Cold War. The Korean conflict, and above all, the Cuban Missile Crisis created in the West an animosity against the Soviet Union and all its satellites. But the images of Soviet troops or KGB methods did not generate the success of anti-Communist movies.

However, the first James Bond films were definitely anti-Soviet and became extraordinarily successful. The production of this phenomenon triggered a lot of spy TV shows (*The Man from U.N.C.L.E.*, *I Spy*, and others that were not too controversial); in addition, for the first three years of *Mission: Impossible*, the episodes were about incidents that took place behind the Iron Curtain. As a matter of fact, the first episode took place on an imaginary Caribbean island (like Cuba), and the main villain physically resembled Fidel Castro. I was surprised that a generally liberal network like CBS would finance and give the green light to such a show, but I learned that Bruce Geller (*Mission: Impossible*'s creator, writer, producer, and director) had been a member of the RAND Corporation's "think tank" during the Korean War, and the episodes dealing with the Iron Curtain were scenarios drawing on that institution's experience.

Furthermore, my own observations helped me to go through a metamorphosis in that field. Although I am not active in politics, I must share with you certain details that might help you to understand my objective position as a social scientist rather than as an emotional activist.

Dizzy Gillespie was very much for African independence. I went with him to meetings in New York City about Angola's civil war in the early sixties. However, after several years he became disappointed with the process in that continent. He finally told me, "The Africans are not ready for independence."

Also, his attitude toward Castro changed from initial sympathy to real antagonism. He went to Cuba several times and after playing and meeting local musicians, he became very active in helping them to escape from the island. Arturo Sandoval, Paquito D'Rivera, Ignacio Berroa, and many others were helped by Dizzy to go into exile.

My own impressions were not different. I saw how many musicians from the Soviet Union and its other satellite countries were members of the several symphony orchestras I conducted all over the world. When I heard the horror stories they told me, I was not surprised, in the end, by the implosion of those regimes and that these artists sought refuge outside their countries.

Notes

1. See also chapter 18.

2. I should add that CBS had commissioned both projects but was going to buy only one.

~

CHAPTER TWENTY-TWO

Film Vignettes

Orson Welles

While working on location (Barcelona, Spain) on the movie *The Voyage of the Damned* in 1975, Faye Dunaway decided to invite the whole cast to a cocktail party in honor of Orson Welles, who was also one of the stars of the project. The party took place at the Ritz Hotel, and Donna and I, the director Stuart Rosenberg and his wife, Malcolm McDowell, Jose Ferrer, and Lee Grant attended it.

Welles was an imposing figure, and he knew how to handle the "center of attention" role extremely well. The first thing he said was that he was occupying the same suite in which Adolf Hitler stayed when he visited Francisco Franco. But he also told stories about his beginnings in show business as a magician in Dublin—which reminded me of Ingmar Bergman's thoughts: "A filmmaker is a magician. Nothing in the film is for real; everything is an illusion."

Orson also remembered (perhaps as our antidote to the former infamous guest of his suite) that during the Second World War he was hired by the British government to make a documentary about the Royal Air Force. He went to London, where he assembled the footage and wrote the narration; before he could finish the project, though, he received a call from Winston Churchill, who needed to show the film that evening after a dinner at his residence. Welles complained that he still needed to add the sound effects and music. Churchill said, "Don't worry, I'll provide the sound effects. Forget about the music for the time being—just do me the favor, please."

Welles was extremely nervous during the dinner, which was attended by members of the cabinet and heads of different branches of the British Armed Forces. In the screening room, when the lights went off and the documentary started with bombs falling onscreen, to Welles's amazement someone in the back was whistling, and whenever there were explosions in the film, incredible noises were created by the mouth of the same whistler. When he turned around in his seat, curious to see who was making the sound effects, he discovered that it was none other than Winston Churchill himself!

Marlon Brando

Rita Moreno, one of the stars of the *West Side Story* film, organized a Christmas party at her residence in 1985. Many celebrities were invited, and Donna and I attended the celebration as well. During the dinner, I was sitting at a table next to Walter Matthau's wife, with whom I was discussing music. All of a sudden, Marlon Brando showed up and sat in the only empty space, next to Mrs. Matthau. I had met Brando back in 1960 in Palm Beach, Florida, when I was touring with Dizzy Gillespie. He obviously did not remember my face, and in the middle of the chatter and party noises, missed hearing my name when we were introduced. However, he paid attention to the musical conversation.

Brando: What are you talking about?

Mrs. Matthau: Mozart.

Brando (to me): Oh, yes? Do you know anything about jazz?

Me: A little.

Brando: Name five jazz drummers.

Me: Max Roach, Buddy Rich, Philly Joe Jones, Mel Lewis, and Grady Tate.

Brando: Who was the drummer known to have a machine-gun style?

Me: Gene Krupa

Brando: Who was Chano Pozo?

Me: A Cuban conga drummer who collaborated with Dizzy Gillespie.

Brando (getting exasperated): What is "nanigo"?

Me: An Afro-Cuban rhythm that is produced by a special kind of drumming, using congas, bongos, timbales, guiro, cowbell, so forth.

Brando (to everyone at the table): Who is this guy?

Gordon Davidson:[1] Marlon, I think this time you are over your head. This is Lalo Schifrin.

Brando: Lalo Schifrin! *(To me)* You really set me up!

I was amused by the incident, and Brando followed me all over after the dinner. He told me he played drums himself, and when I said that I had to leave early because the following morning I had a rehearsal for a Christmas concert, he became very disappointed. Donna and I left before he could make an offer I couldn't refuse. . . .

Henry Mancini

Henry Mancini and I met in London in 1965 while I was working on *The Liquidator* and he was writing the score for another film. Sometimes we had dinner together, and we became friends. That friendship lasted until his death: I still think of him with affection and reverence. He was not only a great composer and songwriter but a lovely man too—very generous, very supportive of younger colleagues, and with a delicious sense of humor. He gave me good advice about the music business in Hollywood, and I still value his experience as well as admiring his music.

During one of our dinners, he told me that after he wrote the score for Blake Edwards's *Breakfast at Tiffany's*, the studio executives watched the complete film put together. After the screening they told Blake Edwards, "It is a good movie, but the frigging song has to go. Just cut it out." The frigging song was "Moon River."

The Cincinnati Kid

When I was hired to write the score for this movie, I was very happy. It was not only a really good movie but also a major one—probably the most important assignment that had come my way at this time

However, I noticed immediately the tension between the director, Norman Jewison, and the producer, Martin Ransohoff. During the spotting session we were interrupted by a phone call to Jewison. He swore and hung up the phone. He made a comment to us about the producer's phone call followed by more profanity. After we finished and he left with the film editor, Hal Ashby, I received a call from Martin Ransohoff's office: the producer wanted to meet me.

The first thing he said to me was "Kid, don't listen to him [Jewison], he doesn't know what the film is about!" The problem was that the two of them had totally different concepts, and they were even fighting about how the movie should end. I realized that I was swimming in dangerous waters. But my instinct for self-preservation kicked in and forced me to do something that I have never again done in my career: I wrote two scores, one for the director and one for the producer. Just in case, I composed *six* different versions for the ending! I worked day and night without sleep; I knew I needed to protect myself in such an important project.

Finally, I showed up at the scoring session. I was so tired that I couldn't conduct. Luckily, Norman Jewison couldn't be there because he was shooting another movie. He sent Hal Ashby[2] to supervise on his behalf; Ransohoff was not present either. As the session started, Ashby noticed that I had scored two different musical versions for each scene. He asked me why. My answer was, "Just in case you need it." The process took longer, but I still did not go overtime.

I carefully avoided showing up at the dubbing session—dialogue, music, sound effects—but a few weeks later I attended a sneak preview in a movie theater of the final film. I wasn't nervous because I hadn't heard any complaints. Nevertheless, once the screening started I realized that my music had been the object of a Solomonic solution: one scene for Jewison, one for Ransohoff, and so forth. One of my six versions of the ending was used, and everybody was happy.

When I told this story to Henry Mancini, he was upset. "That was wrong, you are going to spoil them!" he said. Hank was right: I wish he were still around. But I have never written two scores for the same movie again!

Once a Thief—and Larry Bunker: Los Angeles–Paris, 1965

In 1965 MGM Studios hired me to write the score for a film noir piece, *Once a Thief* with Alain Delon, Ann-Margret, and Jack Palance. The director was Ralph Nelson, who had won the Oscar for *Lilies of the Field* the previous year. The producer was Jacques Bar, the same one I had worked for on *Les Félins* (or *The Joy House*) directed by the French Alfred Hitchcock, Réné Clement.[3]

For *Once a Thief* I needed a symphonic sound integrated with jazz.[4] When I called the contractor, a sort of casting director for musicians, I told him that I needed Larry Bunker as the drummer. Larry's style is subtle, the beat is implied but not hard, and he creates a sort of floating rhythmic pulse that was appropriate for this particular movie. Then, the orchestra was hired and the recording studio booked; I started writing. Two weeks later the MGM contractor called me up and told me that Larry Bunker would not be available for the sessions because he was going on a European tour with Bill Evans. I was disappointed but immediately told him to hire Shelly Manne. So when the time came for the recording session, the music had been thoroughly prepared and the scoring process had gone well.

The second and last recording day, at the lunch break in the MGM Studio restaurant in Culver City, California, I received a phone call from New York. It was Arnold Maxim, the head of MGM Records, Creed Taylor's boss. He told me that I had to fly immediately to London. An MGM film *The Liquidator* had been completed, but its producer, Leslie Elliot, had hired a famous rock band to write the score; it did not fit the movie and was not acceptable to the studio executives. Maxim told me I had very few weeks to compose a new score.

So, after finishing *Once a Thief* I flew to London, where a driver with a white Rolls Royce was waiting for me at the airport. The producer had rented a flat in the exclusive Chelsea section of the British capital and told me that he was at my disposal during my entire stay. I said to him that except for spotting and recording sessions I would not need him during the daytime. That evening I went to Ronnie Scott's jazz club in Soho (with the white Rolls Royce!).

I asked Ronnie's business partner Pete King for references about a "fixer," the UK idiom for "contractor." He said, "I am a fixer," and put together the musicians for me—Tubby Hayes on flute, Ronnie Scott on tenor sax, Tony Crombie on drums, Stan Tracey (the British Thelonious Monk) on piano, plus the BBC Symphony Orchestra. Again, a foretaste of *Jazz Meets the Symphony*.

The whole thing was quite an experience. I was in my flat with a piano, writing music during the day, and every evening the driver of the white Rolls Royce would take me to the club through the narrow streets of Soho.

When the final session took place, including a Shirley Bassey rendition of the title song of *The Liquidator*, everybody was happy, and I proceeded to fly to Paris where Jacques Bar was waiting for me. (Another call from MGM in New York.) He wanted to meet me to talk about an upcoming project.

Once in the French capital, I met some of my old friends and the Argentinean writer Julio Cortazar, who was a kind of disciple of Borges. The streets of the city were covered with posters announcing a forthcoming concert by Bill Evans and his trio at La Maison de la Radio's auditorium. Bill was one of the most influential and innovative pianists in the jazz world, and I and several friends decided we must catch the concert; since right next door to the venue was a restaurant, we decided to have dinner there beforehand.

The restaurant had wooden doors and curtains on the windows that made it impossible to see the interior from the street. We opened the door: sitting at a large table facing it were Bill Evans, Larry Bunker, Chuck Israel (the bassist), and the cream of the Parisian music scene with their wives. They all looked at me and shouted greetings, "Hey, Lalo!" My first words were addressed to Larry Bunker: "Why didn't you want to play for me on *Once a Thief?*"

Larry looked at me, bewildered. He thought I had crossed the whole continent and the Atlantic Ocean just to recriminate him for the MGM cancellation. He thought I'd gone crazy, but when I clarified to everyone at the table my real reason for being in Paris, and the whole thing was an improvised joke, they all relaxed and welcomed me with healthy laughter. Anyway, the concert was magnificent: Bill's brilliant execution of his ideas plus the subtle and unique trio ensemble. It remains one of my more enduring memories.

For some reason, though, Larry Bunker never again canceled any of my scoring sessions in Los Angeles!

The Old Hollywood

John Asher is a gentleman who is a film music connoisseur. His favorite composer was Bernard Herrmann, but after the famous Hitchcock composer had passed away, Asher flew to Los Angeles in order to spend the evening with some of the other composers he admired. He invited to dinner Miklos Rozsa, Bronislau Kaper ("Green Dolphin Street," "Hi Lily Hi Lo"), John Green ("Body and Soul"), and me, representing the younger generation of his favorites on the extensive soundtrack collection he possessed. The venue was Chason's, which was Alfred Hitchcock's favorite restaurant, and they all started to tell stories about the old times in Hollywood. One of them in particular is worth retelling.

Ernest Krenek, one of Schoenberg's disciples, had escaped from Europe during Hitler's evil aggression. Krenek came to Hollywood with his wife and children but no money. He was a highly avant-garde composer, though he had become successful among the intelligentsia in Berlin and Vienna before the Second World War with an opera performed in the "cabaret litteraire" circles. Entitled *Johnny Spielt Auf*, it integrated atonal structure with jazz elements:.

He now sought help from his former professor, and Schoenberg duly called John Green, who at the time was the music director of MGM Studios.

Schoenberg said, "Dr. Krenek can compose, orchestrate, and if necessary work as a copyist or proofreader, but he needs a job." So a delegation of composers under contract with MGM—Green, Rozsa, Kaper, André Previn, and others—went to Irving Thalberg's office (the head of the studio) and told him about Krenek's predicament and how he needed a job.

Thalberg: Is he a composer?

Composers in unison: Yes!

Thalberg: What has he written?

Green: A famous opera, *Johnny Spielt Auf.*

Thalberg: I never heard of it.

Kaper: Have you heard of *La Traviata?*

Thalberg: Did *he* write *La Traviata?*

All: Yessss!!!

Kaper: Have you heard of *Carmen?*

Thalberg: Did *he* write *Carmen?*

All: Yessss!!!

Kaper: Have you heard of *Rigoletto?*

Thalberg: Did *he* write *Rigoletto?*

All: Yessss!!!

By this time, Irving Thalberg was ready to hire Krenek, but the guys went too far.

Kaper: Have you heard of *Cavalleria Rusticana?*

Thalberg: Did *he* write *Cavalleria Rusticana?*

All: Yessss!!!

Thalberg: In that case, I don't want anything to do with this son of a bitch. Just because we used eight bars of *Cavalleria Rusticana* in one of our movies, his publisher is suing us. Out of my office!

So, Ernest Krenek lost his job at MGM Studios. Since he was not only a prolific composer but an analytical writer as well, he should have paid attention to his own essay, "Problems in Opera Style" (1934) before his pals confronted the head of the most venerable studio in Hollywood.

Notes

1. Stage director and the head of all the theaters that belong to the Los Angeles Music Center complex.

2. Ashby was the film's editor; some years later he became a director in his own right, and a very good one.

3. From this picture two music themes originated, "The Cat" and "The Joy House." Both are featured on the Jimmy Smith Verve album *The Cat*.

4. Creed Taylor produced an album *Once a Thief*, but it is not the original sound-track. This was recorded later, half in New York and half in Los Angeles. I remember Phil Woods playing very lyrical lines, with the tone he inherited from Charlie Parker.

PART VI

SYMPHONIC VARIATIONS

CHAPTER TWENTY-THREE

∼

Dies Irae

Hector Berlioz in his memoirs indicates that his *Symphonie Fantastique*, which he wrote when he was very young, was inspired by his desire to portray the life of an artist: his dreams, his loves, his hallucinations, his fears, his aspirations and defeats. The five movements have titles ("Rêveries, Passions," "Un Bal," "Scène aux Champs," "Marche au Supplice," and "Songe d'une Nuit de Sabbat") that reflect his romantic personality. The music is on one hand influenced by the classics but also breaks some rules about the "sonata" form structure. And like all romantics, he was fascinated by the Middle Ages, so he borrowed one of the most famous plainsong melodies, part of the *Requiem Mass* (*Dies Irae*), which expresses terror and fear. In this chapter we are going to visit some episodes of my career, which are also part of my life as an artist. I had some defeats that at the time were disagreeable and some painful. But I never let myself be vanquished by these negative events. My life in music, besides trying to share my joy with my friends and the public, was a constant battle that I had to fight specifically with myself.

In 1968, the executive manager of the Los Angeles Philharmonic approached me. He had been very impressed by my score for the television miniseries *The Rise and Fall of the Third Reich*, based on William Shirer's best-selling book. Mr. Saliers proposed that I write a cantata for soloists, chorus, orchestra, and narration based on my music that would be presented at the Hollywood Bowl. The late British actor Laurence Harvey was going to be the narrator. I came with the idea that the German gods who had been forgotten after the advent of Christianity are plotting to return in order to rule the world. They make

131

a Faustian pact with Satan, who creates his dark angel, Adolf Hitler, to accomplish that sinister mission. The German people are part of the bargain (Goethe's legend is also German), and finally they are defeated and regain their souls by rejecting these kinds of pacts, forever.

The problem was finding someone to write the text. The "librettist" profession has been gradually disappearing—a kind of parallel to Grand Opera's own aging process. To write a libretto is an art different from lyric song writing or poetry. So although I finally found a librettist who had worked on an opera with George Antheil, his final text was mediocre; however, I was so eager to work on the project that I decided to accept it. In order to meet the deadline there was no time to talk about changes, and besides, there was no way in which this problem could be fixed. My collaborator had the technique, but his ideas were obsolete.

Despite all this, my inspired determination enabled me to write a score in which I displayed my composition and orchestration devices with imagination and conviction. But I had forgotten that music and words should be integrated in an organic and functional way,[1] and I paid the price for that amnesia when *The Rise and Fall of the Third Reich* was premiered at the Hollywood Bowl. Even during the rehearsals I realized that things weren't working; I was particularly aware of how I had managed to underline some of the libretto's clichés in my own writing. Sensing already that the whole thing was bound for disaster, I should have withdrawn my music from the event then and there, but I lacked the courage to do so.

The final result was a failure so big that I wanted to leave town. However, although I couldn't face myself in the aesthetic mirror, a new commission came from the Los Angeles Philharmonic in 1971. Zubin Mehta, who was the music director, wanted me to write a major work for a jazz band and orchestra. This was a great opportunity for me to erase the memories of my defeat.

But instead of following my instinct, which advised me to cultivate the garden that I had already started with the *Marquis De Sade* and *Bullitt* and the seeds of what became *Jazz Meets the Symphony*, I unfortunately chose another path. I ignored my feelings and used only my intellect, persuading myself that as avant-garde classical music and free jazz have so many things in common, I could combine the aleatory technique of orchestral music with the atonal language of Archie Shepp, Ornette Coleman, and Don Cherry.

The piece was entitled *Music for Jazz Band, Electronic Keyboard and Orchestra*. The band was very good: together with some veterans like Ray Brown, Larry Bunker, Jack Nimitz, and Conte Candoli, I hired some young soloists who played "free" jazz; I also decided to play the Yamaha-provided electronic instruments myself.

There were high expectations from the music community and the public. Yamaha organized a publicity machine, which mirrored the technical perfection of their products. But the end result of the world premiere was another disaster. Although I had arranged a conversation between the band, the orchestra, and my Yamaha monster, to my chagrin I realized that I had become as a sorcerer's apprentice. Things got out of hand. I did not have enough experience to manipulate the electronic keyboards and different sounds for a live concert. And the free jazz musicians had no idea of the composition's proportions, so their solos were overly extended. The whole piece itself was too long, not only difficult to understand but also "hard to listen to," as Dizzy Gillespie had said about a European language spoken in one of the countries in which we had performed. The classical reviewer of the *Los Angeles Times* blasted me, as did Leonard Feather, and rightly so: I had made the biggest mistake that an artist can possibly commit, creating a work that was not based on my natural development and instincts but a pastiche to "épater les bourgeois." Dadaism, Theatre of Cruelty, and surrealism were obsolete and I was not even good at these forms, since this was not what I had to say.

However, after many years, Zubin Mehta not only forgave me but became very enthusiastic about what I was doing with *Jazz Meets the Symphony*. He wanted me, on four different occasions, to guest conduct tours with the Israel Philharmonic, and he is now planning to do the same with the orchestra of the Florence (Italy) Opera. He was my biggest champion with the Three Tenors and was kind enough to recommend me to the Sultan of Oman for a commission.[2]

Those two episodes are fully my responsibility, and I have nobody to blame but myself. And I've learned from my mistakes.

Notes

1. Some years later, a very well-known jazz singer told me that he was recording a song of mine because he liked the music but not the lyrics. To my mind, this made the whole song a failure.

2. See chapters 28 and 32.

CHAPTER TWENTY-FOUR

~

Scales and Arpeggios

By the late 1980s, despite the occasional breakouts to play "live" jazz and increased baton work, either with *Jazz Meets the Symphony* or as a guest conductor of various symphony orchestras, classical commissions were beginning to compete for my time with my annual quota of movie scores. Already behind me in this field were *Canons for String Quartet*, premiered by the Los Angeles String Quartet, and other chamber pieces; a choral work, *They Shall Not Make War Anymore*; and—even more prestigious—commissioned by Jascha Heifetz and Gregor Piatigorsky, a double concerto for violin, cello, and orchestra.

In 1990 came a recording by the Dorian Wind Quintet on Summit Records of my *La Nouvelle Orléans*, a seven-minute work juxtaposing an elaborated primitivism with what might be called "universal thoughts." I have contemplated the principle of renewal as expressed by the Chinese philosopher and founder of Taoism, Lao-tzu ("Be worn and you will remain new"); by the astronomer Carl Sagan ("Death is the secret of evolution"); and in an old New Orleans saying, "Eleven macks a-ridin' to the graveyard but only ten a-coming back." The title of the piece symbolizes the advent of the new emerging from the old. Benefiting from an immaculate performance, the music is redolent with sustained sonorities, with different solo instruments darting their figures above and around these sustains. These gradually turn into a semi-bluesy New Orleans funeral march, with Sidney Bechet or Edmond Hall leading the procession . . . except that it's the Dorian Wind Quintet's own Jerry Kirkbride playing the evocative clarinet!

Released in 1993, by Label X, *Continuum/Journeys/Voyage* is an update of music I had composed in the 1970s. *Continuum* was commissioned by the American Harp Society and premiered in Houston, Texas, by Anne Stockton, who later recorded it for Avant Records.[1] The piece was conceived as a continuous flowing of sound undergoing gradually different disturbances that change in a subtle way the whole structure of that flow. After so many "events" and so many changes, the cycle of the music returns to its beginnings. The shape and nature of *Continuum* were dictated by the nature of the harp itself, as well as the possibilities and impossibilities that are part of the instrument's technology. This is music I could never have written for the piano or any other instrument.

Journeys was composed in 1973 for Ken Watson, one of the leading percussionists in the United States, and premiered in 1976. It incorporates almost all the main percussion instruments—plus such exotica as maracas, bongos, crotales, and the strings of a prepared piano across which wire brushes and a mallet are drawn.

There is a sort of choreography to this piece in which the soloist alternates the execution of a number of fixed (static) groups with relatively free-motion-around (kinetic) performances. Six different copies of the score should be placed at fixed groups. The soloist should assemble the maximum number of instruments on the transitional paths, leaving open paths from one fixed group to another in such a way that would enable him or her to play on the right and left. The transitions are very free but should continue a logical sequence from group to group. The selection of instruments for the parts should be limited by availability of natural ringing instruments. (Try to avoid dampened or quickly decaying sounds.) The actual performance during the transitional sections should be walking and moving constantly along the "paths" until a new fixed group is reached. This process is indicated via "transition path" or "travel to" and so forth.

Journeys begins with just wind chimes and vibraphone before moving on to Chinese gong and crash cymbal; then tubular bells and tympani; then virtually everything else in the percussion department—even glockenspiel and Asiatic drums. That certainly tested Ken Watson over twenty-three minutes—but triumphantly, for both player and his composer. However, its groupings of instruments must have proved merry devils for the recording engineer!

Voyage is the integrated suite for chamber orchestra based on the music I had written for the film *Voyage of the Damned*. The cimbalom is played on this recording by John Leach.

In 1995 I found a very good reason to return to my Latin American roots, but still in a classical way. I was invited to write a piece featuring the gifted Mexican flutist Marisa Canales. This led to *Three Tangos*, issued as part of her *Music from the Americas* album between a concerto for flute and small orchestra and a sonata for flute and piano by her compatriot composer Samuel Zyman. As is clear from the outset, my tangos are not those of popular romantic conception, but a bridge between Astor Piazzolla's modernism and European classical techniques. The dream-like quality of the second one especially has more in common with Debussy's *Prelude à l'Après-Midi d'Un Faune* than the dance hall (albeit with a certain starkness of phrasing grafted on), while the rhythmic *pizzicato* string accompaniment in one passage during the third gravitates closely toward Stravinsky's *The Rite of Spring*.

Partly because of Marisa Canales's superb playing, that tango commission encouraged me to explore further the flute's potentialities, thus inspiring the *Concierto Caribeño for Flute and Orchestra* of 1997. Its three movements cover a blanket spectrum of what the musical term *Latin* can mean: from South America to the Caribbean Islands, and even encompassing the imported elegance of Old Spain and the Mediterranean. All these idioms are deployed either to underpin, or engage in orchestral dialogues with, the sheer virtuosity of Marisa Canales's flute as she dazzles and sings through a myriad of contrasting passages. The rhythmic tapestry is equally varied and complex, reminding one of how much Africa as well as the conquistadores have influenced the New World.

The work was recorded with the backing of the London Symphony Orchestra. And I coupled it with my *Concerto for Guitar and Orchestra* dating from 1985, the soloist on this occasion being Juan Carlos Laguna, also Mexican by birth and winner of the 1991 Tokyo International Guitar Competition. The score has been described as a *fantasia concertante* on account of its rich tonal palette and the way in which, after the initial military fanfare (a reminder of Spain's Golden Age), instead of the orchestra merely accompanying, the soloist enters into a series of fascinating duets with individual instruments or sections of players. Laguna even "serenades" the full orchestra at one point.

I employ what is known as a Landini cadence as a fulcrum to give the opening movement its overall stylistic unity. In the busy second, Laguna takes us into the heart of the jungle—including echoes of Messiaen with its birdsong. And the third merges Latin America with Old Europe again: Spanish Renaissance dance music evolving into a rhythmic coat of many colors as it is absorbed by its own overseas Empire. The recording (on Auvidis) also includes the thirteen-minute *Trópicos*, a suite in five brief movements for woodwind quintet and strings. This is deliberately realist tone-painting, though with vigorous, built-in rhythms. Nevertheless, as it progresses every instrument gets to be a soloist.

Finally, recorded by Aleph Records in 1988 and reissued in 1999, there is the *Lalo Schifrin Conducts Stravinsky, Schifrin and Ravel* collection—made in France at the Champs-Élysées Theatre with the Paris Philharmonic Orchestra. I get to conduct two of my favorite works: Stravinsky's ballet *Petrouchka* and Ravel's *Ma Mére l'Oye*, better known to us as the *Mother Goose Suite*, ending with its almost painfully beautiful ballad for strings, *Le Jardin Féerique* (or *Fairy Garden*).

In between is my opus, *Concerto for Bass and Orchestra* in three movements. It was commissioned in January 1986 by the virtuoso double bassist Gary Karr, and he asked for it be as lyrical as possible: "I would like to make the instrument sing," he said. Immediately I decided to write a concerto in the shape of an opera, where the double bass would be the *basso* protagonist. As a musician of European ancestry but born in Latin America, I had become fascinated a few years before by the discovery that a composer like Antonio Vivaldi had written an opera about the Aztec emperor/god Montezuma. Obviously, my "opera" did not have a story, but the Montezuma/Vivaldi connection triggered an imaginary musical idiom based on neo-Baroque and Indo-American elements. I was compelled by the idea of alternating colorful scenes ("dances," "choruses") with introspective arias, recitatives, and duets.

However, the challenge was to give an internal unity to the many elements and at the same time create a showcase for the solo instrument. Like Europeans exploring *terra incognita*, I sailed through the strings of the bass. Gary himself, prodigiously skilled with both bow and finger, helped me with a catalog of possible extensions, figurations, bowing techniques, and articulations that I proceeded to integrate into the work, and for the performance he played the famous 1611 Amati double bass given to him by the widow of Serge Koussevitzky.

In the final analysis, the double bass does not portray the characters of Montezuma or Vivaldi so much as the subjective impressions of a modern observer attempting to interpret the interdependence of particular historical events and searching his own soul while reviewing parades of orchestral timbres, joining their rhythms and "singing" along with their melodic contours.

Note

1. Owned, coincidentally, by Lester Remsen, husband of Dorothy Remsen, who plays it on the Label X recording.

CHAPTER TWENTY-FIVE

~

Fantasy for Screenplay and Orchestra

The work is music for an imaginary film. Listeners are invited to create their own storylines and their own visual images as they react to different moods suggested by the music's flow. Its overall structure is borrowed from Mussorgsky's *Pictures at an Exhibition*: my "pictures" are motion pictures, and my "exhibition" is furnished by movie theater owners, who are known as exhibitors.

I. *Main Title* (or *Overture*) contains the principal theme, which is based on six-note motifs that pose two questions. The strings and woodwind are in charge of the responses. A change of tempo gives way to a more agitated version of the theme, with the intervention of the full orchestra and the introduction of the second theme. Echoes of the six-note motifs bring this *Main Title* section to a quiet ending. The sound of the last sustained chord by the diminuendo strings fades out gradually: the equivalent of a visual "dissolve."

II. *Film Noir.* This section could be interpreted as a nightmare or the music for a thriller. The elements of menace, suspense, tension, and shock are the ingredients. An alto flute solo accompanied by a double bass *pizzicato* contributes to enhancing the atmosphere of mystery. If there was a crime, perhaps it was solved; or we slowly awaken from the dark dream.

III. *First Transition.* A variation on the main theme, this time introduced by the principal French horn as a bridge to the next scene.

IV. *The Silent Comedians.* One of the main elements of film music is the audiovisual counterpoint. I have written the score for a movie, *Rollercoaster,* in which an extortionist destroys amusement parks with bombs. The music of the innocent merry-go-rounds, calliopes, and children's rides plays against the horror of the images on the screen—not unlike the circus clown in Andreyev's story *He Who Gets Slapped*, whose inner tragedy is in contrast to his painted-on smile. Again, this orchestral journey can be taken as a farcical statement. Its simple naiveté in waltz tempo, which may lead to an absurd chase, could also be the counterpoint to something abominable that happens on the screen.

V. *Second Transition.* Another orchestration of the principal theme. This "promenade" ends with bells and takes us to the next sequence.

VI. *Love Scene.* Many elements that express the most important bonds between two people (attraction, doubt, jealousy, and passion) are reflected in the music, which searches for a sensual tango rhythm to accompany the many faces of love.

VII. *The Final Conflict.* Trombones, bassoons, and percussion announce the coming battle in the form of a fugue of different sonorities and a montage of violent scenes that lead to the triumphal and heroic ending, with the final transformation of the principal theme. And as the last sound is followed by silence, the last "image" is followed by the "dark screen." The silence is important, but what "happened" on the screen was an illusion.

~

CHAPTER TWENTY-SIX

The Triple Concerto

This was commissioned by the Halcyon Trio. In essence it's a comprehensive *étude* of the possible interplay between the solo ensemble and an orchestra comprising only a brass choir and a full string section. [The piano in its higher octaves and the clarinet can easily replace the woodwind grouping. And again the piano can create percussive effects or become a substitute for the harp.]

The first movement—which I've called *The Age of Anxiety*—starts off with a "classica" rhythmic figure prevalent in the be-bop era of jazz. Besides which, the intervals are based on a twelve-tone row and its retrogradation. The figure exposed by the trio is a *passacaglia*. Subtle pyramids by the strings and fast punctuations by the trumpets contribute to a gradual build. The trio is joined by double basses (*pizzicato*) and low brass. A tumultuous climax results by different counterpoints also based on be-bop phrases. The tension keeps building until the trio asserts itself through a second section, always "exploring" their jazz-inspired figures on top of the *passacaglia* (which continues via the piano's left hand). A dramatic intervention by the horns, tuba, and strings breaks into this previous mood. A third section based loosely on blues motifs serves as an introduction to the movement's second theme, more diatonic but extending the scales by a free use of intervals of fourths and fifths. A developing section of the second theme allows the different possibilities of alternate and simultaneous interaction between all the players. Such a musical procedure brings forth another buildup to the three individual cadenzas by the soloists. A short recapitulation of the *passacaglia* leads to a quiet end to the movement.

The second movement is intended as a calm antidote to *The Age of Anxiety*. A melodic, neo-Baroque theme with accompaniment of the string *ostinato* figure expresses a lyrical mood, which stretches almost into a new romantic idiom. A second theme (*lied*) emerges, exposed by the clarinet and accompanied first by the piano and then by the viola and double basses. After an expanding development, it triggers three variations featuring the possibilities of technical displays by the soloists and the orchestra. A short triple cadenza precedes the calm recapitulation of the first theme. The coda slowly evanesces into distant echoes.

Excitement is the key word to describe the third and final movement! An introduction by the brass playing syncopated figures announces a short motif by the strings. This motif is the essence of the first theme, and, again, the language of modern jazz permeates this whole movement.

The development by canonic figures, transformations, extensions, and contractions is interrupted by the syncopated brass. The solo viola introduces a second theme, more lyrical, but the nervous pulse continues to push the music forward. This theme is also subjected to different developments. A new translation brings back the syncopated figure. The soloists respond with an ostinato based on African rhythms. The first motif of the first theme starts announcing itself. A short French horn "call" introduces a *fugato* by the strings, who re-expose the theme.

New developments take place. The piano dialogues with the other two soloists accompanied by the orchestra. The theme goes back through many transformations and builds to the cadenzas by clarinet, viola, and piano. This last instrument connects at the end of its solo with the final coda. The initial motif, the "impetus," has the last word with a sense of affirmation. This ending does not pose a question; rather it becomes a reiteration of the celebratory spirit of the whole concerto.

[Note: *The Triple Concerto* has not yet been recorded.]

CHAPTER TWENTY-SEVEN

~

Cantos Aztecas

The discovery of the Inca and pre-Inca civilizations in Peru had a big impact on my emotions. I developed an invisible bond with populations that I only studied in history books, and now I could feel their lasting impressions as a patrimony of mankind. A visit to Machu Picchu, Cuzco, the archeological museum in Lima, allowed me to discover something that came from the past but at the same time touched my present emotions—like the discovery of the three feathers of the Inca emperor, which had colors that exist neither in nature nor in the paintings of the greatest European masters. Their music based on pentatonic scales has a haunting quality, and their monuments and masks keep a secret mystery that I've tried to decipher.

Years later, during my travels to Mexico, I also visited the anthropological museum in Mexico City, and again I felt the contact with the Indo-American culture. My visit to the pyramids of the Teotihuacan prompted an intense reaction that did not go unnoticed by my friend, Benjamin Juarez, an associate director of the Philharmonic Orchestra of Mexico City. A great supporter of my music, he was instrumental in securing me several invitations to conduct and several commissions, including my *Piano Concert No. 1*. Knowing my passion for pre-Colombian civilizations, he encouraged me to write a cantata for voices and orchestra based on ancient Aztec poems that I had come upon at the anthropological museum; those written by an Aztec prince of the twelfth century particularly captured my imagination, and I'd felt I could put music into their inspiring metaphors and images.

Benjamin proposed that the project should include the orchestra and the chorus at the theater where they regularly perform their concerts. I rejected the idea: my vision was to present the *Cantos Aztecas* at the archeological site of Teotihuacan with four soloists (soprano, tenor, contralto, bass) plus the chorus and the orchestra. Everybody thought I was crazy. The son of an ex-president of Mexico who was also a composer told me to put aside such a fantasy: he wanted to do a concert at the same venue when his father was in office, but he had not been allowed to.

Anyway, during those days, I had to conduct a series of concerts at the Mexico City Theater (Teatro de la Ciudad de México). At the end of the last concert the standard procedure of signing autographs took place, a line of the concert-goers with programs parading outside my dressing room. They all looked like the average classical music lovers, of European extraction. But the last person in the line was a short old Indian lady, modestly attired. Her name was Klautzin, and full of emotion she said to me, "Please write something that would honor the Nahuatl culture." I was astonished since our *Cantos Aztecas* project had not yet been announced. She gave me a brochure of a society that preserves the tradition of the Mesomexico tribes. The brochure ended with a poem by Nexahualcoyotl, and after her departure I put it in my briefcase with the rest of my scores and batons. The following day, Benjamin took me to a special bookstore where he got for me a Nahuatl-Spanish dictionary and a Nahuatl grammar and syntax. I had decided to write the *Cantos* in the Aztecs' original language.

In the meantime, my obsession to present the work in Teotihuacan remained as strong as ever. The site is known as "the city of the gods," as according to the legend, the gods had a convention in one of its temples and decided to create the world. The place is awesome. A large and long avenue half a mile wide runs for three miles, flanked by ruins of the temples, pyramids, and homes. At the two extremes of this impressive artery (known as the Avenue of Death) are two gigantic monuments, the Pyramid of the Sun and the Pyramid of the Moon. It is a dramatic spectacle beyond the conception of any stage director.

However, the orchestra and friends tried to explain that a live performance on the archeological site would be too expensive. There were no seats for the audience, no facilities; the orchestra and chorus would have to be paid extra for traveling one hour away from Mexico City; a stage needed to be built and a sound system incorporated. The whole production would be too expensive. Nevertheless, I did not give up. I thought that Placido Domingo would be the perfect tenor to portray the author of the *Cantos*, and when I mentioned this idea they could see that I really was determined, for the additional cost of his fees raised the overall budget to US$2 million.

As soon as I came back to L.A., I started to write the score at a feverish speed. By coincidence, Benjamin Juarez came to Los Angeles where he had a conducting engagement. He stayed at my house, and on his return from rehearsals every evening, he was astonished by the daily progress I was making. The number of pages rose geometrically. My handwriting had changed, and it was almost as if I were possessed by the Aztec gods. As soon as I finished, I sent the score to Placido Domingo. After a few days, he called me and said that he liked it and wanted to talk to me about it. "Let's meet in Acapulco for Easter."[1]

At that meeting he proposed the other members of the cast—Conchita Julian (soprano), Martha Felix (contralto), and Nikita Storojev (bass). Then Jose Juan Bertagni, an Argentinean engineer, joined us: he had invented a "transducer"—a screen that became the loudspeaker with a very natural sound. At once, the doors started to open. American Express became our sponsor: that year was the twenty-fifth anniversary of the green card in Mexico, and they were looking for an event to celebrate the occasion. The sound team from the Hollywood Bowl was hired, as was a visual effects company from San Francisco to assist Bertagni. The Mexican authorities made a condition that whatever works had to be made at the site must not damage the original stone, so archeologists were engaged to help the building of the stage and the seats for the audience. The police from the state of Mexico provided the security, and the catering for a reception for one thousand VIPs after the concert was funded by Maxim's.

Meanwhile, Placido was meeting me in my house, or at the Metropolitan Opera in New York, to rehearse and prepare his performance. It was a joy to work with him, and not just because of his musicality and the sublime way his voice interpreted my music: he also understood my ideas instinctively and indeed nourished them. At one point, he suggested that the first half of the concert should be by the orchestra only, performing works by Mexican composers (Moncayo, Chavez, Revueltas). He also argued that since *Cantos Aztecas* was a world premiere, to be attended by twelve thousand people, with VIPs paying US$1,000 a ticket, we should finish the concert with a new work using twentieth-century techniques. He said, "I am sure everything will be all right, but just in case let's give the public a safe ending. Why don't you write for me an arrangement of 'Granada'?" Respecting his "show business" experience, I agreed. The last thing to determine was the date: American Express wanted it during October, so Placido chose the last Saturday of the month. Everything was now set in motion.

However, I was agonizing somewhat because I wanted to change the ending of the *Cantos*. The Aztec prince's poetry was very moving, sometimes celebrating, magical, even psychedelic, but for the very end I needed a simple universal concept. His lyrical, more intimate lines were rather depressing philosophical expressions about the futility of human endeavor—which was not good for the work's finale. All of a sudden I remembered the brochure that the Indian lady, Klautzin, had given me in Mexico City. I went to my briefcase and there it was: "We do not know why we come to this earth, what is the meaning of all this, but it cannot be in vain. Let us leave at least some flowers, let us leave at least some songs."—Nexahualcoyotl. These beautiful lines were the key for the last part of the *Cantos*, and my changed ending was fulfilled.

Meanwhile, I'd made several trips to Mexico in order to attend various receptions to explain to potential audiences what the whole thing was about. I also visited Teotihuacan, where the archeologists had found a stone platform next to the Pyramid of the Moon where the musicians used to perform during the empire of the Mexican tribes. This is where the stage for the orchestra, chorus, and soloists would be built with cranes in order not to damage the original stone.

I also tried through American Express to contact Mrs. Klautzin, who had given me her address and phone number along with the brochure. We called her but her number had been changed; we sent drivers to her place, but she had moved without leaving a forwarding address. This was very frustrating to me because I wanted to share with her the anticipated experience.

Anyway, after several trips to and fro-ing between Los Angeles and Mexico, the final week came before the event. I went back to direct the rehearsals. The schedule was very tight since we worked with the orchestra in the mornings, with the choir in the afternoons, and with the soloists in the evening. Slowly the results of such dedicated work started to pay off, and the piece started to come together.

By this time the twelve thousand tickets were completely sold out. Placido Domingo was frustrated because he wanted to bring a jet-load of his European fans from Luxor, where he had just performed *Aida*. I had to appear on an early live television show "Good Morning Mexico." At the end of the interview I asked the host if he would allow me a personal message. I faced the camera and said: "Mrs. Klautzin, wherever you are, I would like to invite you to attend the concert this coming Saturday. I will leave two tickets for you at the reception of the Camino Real Hotel in your name."

The day before the world premiere, Placido Domingo arrived by helicopter from Mexico City, and we played through the whole repertoire on the

Teotihuacan stage, including the "Granada" encore. In the evening, we had a dress rehearsal with the screens, sound transducers, and lights, with the television director following the score in order to get the right shots. All of a sudden, Mrs. Klautzin appeared and gave me a hug. She was very moved. I asked her how she knew about the dress rehearsal. "When the gods are involved, I always know."

Finally, D-day arrived. I tried to hide my tension; with so many pieces on the board, anything could go wrong. Before I left my hotel, the concierge confirmed that Mrs. Klautzin's daughter had picked up the tickets. When I arrived with my family and friends at Teotihuacan, I was stupefied by what greeted my eyes—the new stage, the sound system, the enormous outdoor theater packed with people, the screens, the TV cameras, and the sound engineers in charge of recording the live performance for a CD, which my Eric Alberts had flown in from Paris to produce. All of a sudden I thought, "My God, everything will be dismantled tomorrow, with the workers, the cranes, the different technicians in charge of deconstructing my dream." I felt like Fellini toward the end of 8 1/2: "Perhaps all this is for nothing."

The seats assigned to Mrs. Klautzin were in a good section, but my wife, Donna, was right in front of the stage. Next to her was the only empty seat in the whole place, which Mrs. Klautzin suddenly occupied with gracious self-assurance. Donna said, "I am sorry but the whole place is sold out and somebody may still claim this seat." "Nobody is coming," answered Mrs. Klautzin. At 8:00 p.m. I went to the stage and proceeded to conduct the first half of the concert. The musicians were wonderful: the Mexico Philharmonic had American players for the woodwind section; some string players from Russia, Ukraine, and Poland; and two Bulgarian harpists. The rest of the orchestra—the brass, the majority of strings, and the percussion—were Mexicans. The three pieces in the first half went well, and the public showed their appreciation with a warm applause.

But now the main focus of the evening was to come. By this time the black velvet of the night covered Teotihuacan. The stars were shining and a full moon was illuminating the stage and the crowd behind the Pyramid of the Moon: talk about Latin American magic realism! Mrs. Klautzin came backstage, and in front of the soloists and me she addressed the heavens: "Can you imagine, mother, that a major work in the Nahuatl language is going to be performed by these artists?"[2] She then made an invocation to the Aztec gods and gave us her benediction.

We went onto the stage, and from the moment the music began, we all felt a mystic connection. I had to concentrate on the score, giving cues to musicians and singers. The chorus of the Mexico City Orchestra was perfect, and their voices reflected the different moods of the piece. I was also aware all the time that this was a live recording, and no mistakes were allowed. Then, after the final chord, there was an instant of total silence. I thought, "That's it, a failure." But immediately the audience broke into a standing ovation. We took bows, and I stopped counting the times we returned to the stage after nineteen. The audience kept standing, screaming with joy and cries of "Bravo!" from all over. While we were taking one of the bows I discreetly asked Placido Domingo if we should do the encore "Granada." He said, "No: let us not destroy this magical moment."

Needless to say, tears came to my eyes. I never dreamed that we would enjoy this kind of triumph, and flashbacks of all the difficulties, impediments, and efforts passed through my mind while the audience went on hailing us with such warmth: it was, simply, one of the greatest moments in my life. I congratulated the magnificent soloists, Conchita Julian, Martha Felix, Nikita Storojev, Placido Domingo, and the choral director, whom I invited to take bows with us. But although the moon was still rotating and the stars shining, Mrs. Klautzin had disappeared.

We performed the *Cantos Aztecas* in Paris, and there were productions in the United States by the San Antonio Symphony. However, I never heard again from Mrs. Klautzin. Somebody told me recently that she passed away, but I'll never forget that she helped me to "leave at least some flowers, some songs."

Notes

1. This was 1989.
2. When Mrs. Klautzin was a child, her father forbade her family the use of the native language. Only through Spanish one could advance in Mexican society. Incidentally, too, Nahuatl is not a dead language: it is spoken by two million people. During the Second World War, Mexican American pilots confronting their Japanese enemy communicated in Nahuatl. The Japanese were unable to break the code.

CHAPTER TWENTY-EIGHT

⌐

The Three Tenors and the Opera World

After the *Cantos Aztecas* concert, a dinner for the one thousand VIPs took place in a Spanish convent a few miles from the pyramids' site. The convent was built in the sixteenth century by the conquerors of Mexico. I thought this was ironic. In my mind this was no different from a reception in the Gestapo headquarters after a musical event for the victims of the Holocaust.[1] Be that as it may, the party was very animated, with decorated tables, parading waiters, singing mariachis, enormous quantities of food, champagne, and good wines, and I felt very happy with the success of my work. So I joined in the spirit of the party.

Placido Domingo, his family, and his friends were sitting at the next table, and later we sat together for a while. He was very pleased, observing that the Aztec mythology was richer than the Wagnerian one and that I should consider writing an opera based on it. I then remembered "Granada" and told him that I had no use for the arrangement, so it would be a pleasure for me to offer it to him. He graciously accepted my gift and instructed me to send it to his office in New York City. A few months later he performed it at the Met for the New Year's Eve concert with the New York Philharmonic conducted by Zubin Mehta.

At the beginning of 1990 I was contacted by Gaston Fournier, who was the general director of the Florence Opera. A big event was going to take place on the eve of the final game of the football (soccer) World Cup that year in the Thermes of Caracalla in Rome. For the first time the three superstar opera tenors, Jose Carreras, Placido Domingo, and Luciano Pavarotti, were going to perform together with the opera orchestras of Rome and Florence. Fournier asked me to write the orchestrations, since no score written for three tenors and an orchestra exists in the whole history of music literature.

I was intrigued by the challenge. When my father took me as a child to the opera performances in Buenos Aires, I found it curious that opera singers without microphones could perform above the orchestra. When I started to study scores, especially those of Verdi, Bizet, and Debussy, I discovered that those composers accompanied the voices in a subtle way and sometimes in the dramatic climaxes there were tutti effects like aural mirages. The percussion and brass played the accents, but the woodwinds stayed a little longer and started to disappear, and only the strings remained for the rest of the passage. The audience hears the tutti ensemble fortissimo but is not aware of the paring down of the orchestral texture. Of course, other composers like Wagner use a bigger orchestra, demanding very powerful voices, and in most cases the conductor has to control the balance.

I had already solved those problems in my own way in the *Cantos Aztecas*. But here, although once again the event was going to take place outdoors with the use of microphones and amplification, the challenge was to write the arrangements using opera techniques. I wanted to create an aural atmosphere that would be as close as possible to the world in which the three soloists would feel comfortable. I set up a meeting in Paris with Fournier and the show's producer, Mario Dradi. I was due to conduct concerts and recordings in the French capital, so we decided to get together for lunch at the Hotel Plaza Athenee, where I was staying.

The restaurant had a stage where a band consisting of violin (the leader), saxophone, trumpet, piano, guitar, bass, and drums was playing light music. We sat as far as possible from the bandstand so that we could talk. They told me that the medley I was supposed to write was the grand finale of the concert. Prior to that, the three tenors would take turns singing solo opera arias or songs.[2] And that turned out to be the key of the medley's presentation. A method of rotation was devised, one of my tasks being to give each one of the superstars equal time in front of the TV cameras and the live audience;[3] Zubin Mehta would conduct both orchestras together.

Then we talked about the repertoire. Fournier and Dradi brought a list of songs that might be included; that was their right and their job, but I had my own ideas of how they should be programmed, and coming up with a solution that satisfied all of us was starting to prove problematic, until I had an inspiration. I went to the bandstand and gave the violinist leader several hundred francs to play two or three songs in a certain order. Then Mario

Dradi gave the members of the band more tips, experimenting with how the musical numbers flowed one after the other. By the end of the lunch we had completed the order of the grand finale medley!

Afterward, Mario Dradi said that before becoming an opera producer, he had been an archeologist. I could not help thinking that I was a kind of musical archeologist. In this case I remembered that as a child, on occasions when my parents took me to attend opera performances at the Teatro Colon in Buenos Aires, the soloists were singing some of the same songs as encores: "O Sole Mio," "Mattinata," "Amapola," "O Paese d' 'o Sole." They were still in my memory.

Back in my home in Los Angeles while writing the orchestrations, I realized that I was now entering a new territory. I had already immersed myself in jazz lore without even trying, playing and writing for some of the legendary figures of that music. I also had taken a place in the film and television world by working with some of the great directors and famous stars, and I had succeeded in the world of classical music as well. Now I was engaging the operatic tradition. And in each genre, my profound interest in and attraction to history was fundamental, the driving force behind what I wanted to express in music.

There was no sense of vanity in these reflections, but instead a realization of the tremendous sense of responsibility they implied. My fascination with history led me to write an opera for Placido Domingo, *The Trial of Louis the XVI* (*Le Procès de Louis Capet*). Wherever my activities took me I was compelled to visit museums and historical and archeological sites. Even the darkest periods of recent times evoked strong impressions. A skinhead demonstration in Vienna, while working with Jose Carreras, brought a horrible recreation of Nazi brutality to my vivid imagination. Or in Berlin (while with Julia Migenes, who was the protagonist as singer and actress in the movie *Carmen* together with Placido Domingo), when contemplating the infamous wall, I could not stop thinking about the gulags and the Stalinistic terror. These images were so vivid that I felt overwhelmed by them.

But back to music. I was finding a sanctuary where I felt protected enough to keep exploring the labyrinths of time and to pursue my need to know where everything was coming from. So far some of the results had been *Gillespiana*, *Marquis de Sade*, and *Cantos Aztecas*, and *Jazz Meets the Symphony* was just around the corner. But aside from this introspection, the music for the three tenors was completed. The concert in Rome was extremely successful, and the number of CDs and videos sold surpassed all the records in the classical category.

My collaboration with Mario Dradi continued in two Christmas in Vienna events. One concert was with Diana Ross, Placido Domingo, and Jose Carreras. The other was with the same tenors and Natalie Cole. Also, Jose Carreras asked me to write and conduct a CD for him, which started in Vienna and was completed in London and Hamburg. The last time Dradi (the archeologist) approached me was to propose a challenging project: I was offered the opportunity to write a cantata for famous opera stars (among them the baritone Ruggiero Raimondi), a chorus, and an orchestra to celebrate the 3,000th anniversary of Jerusalem. The event was going to take place outdoors in the Sultan's Pool of the city. The Israel Philharmonic and chorus plus the soloists were under the direction of Zubin Mehta. The idea was to render tribute to the city that is so important for the three monotheistic religions: Judaism, Christianity, and Islam.

My music was supposed to be ecumenical, all-encompassing, and expressing the ideas of peace, unity, and hope. The text was chosen from the *Psalms*: once again, history was knocking at my door. However, an unfortunate incident happened in the pre-compositional stages. Although from my ethnomusicology studies I knew something about Arab music, I needed to get closer to their religious music. I called Dr. Edward Said, the Near East specialist at Columbia University Arabic Studies department in New York, for help. Being a Palestinian Arab (although he had been born in Egypt) he was mistrustful, and obviously he did not want to cooperate with the Israeli government. He told me that in Islam there is no such thing as religious music, only chants. I found out much later that there is indeed liturgical music in the Islamic religion: the truth is that Dr. Said refused to help me, period.

In order to be loyal to the authenticity and solemnity of the project, I asked for translations of the *Psalms* into Hebrew, Aramaic, Latin, Greek, and Arabic, though Dradi insisted the text be in English.[4] Anyway, I wrote the work as initially projected, and it was performed as such. The performance by the orchestra and the chorus was impeccable, and the public seemed very much to enjoy it. Zubin had done his homework, and he is without a doubt one of the greatest conductors of our time. The soloists came somewhat unprepared since their schedules didn't allow them the time to study a new work. But the final result was quite good. My publisher tells me that the *Psalms* is one of my most sought out compositions. A video from the live performance telecast is in existence.

In 1994, the football (soccer) World Cup took place in the United States. The Three Tenors got together for a second time at Dodger Stadium in Los Angeles on the eve of the final game. This time the producer was Tibor

Rudas, who happened to manage Luciano Pavarotti as well. One year before the event I had a meeting in New York with the three soloists, their agents, lawyers, Zubin Mehta, Tibor Rudas, and his assistants. While planning the whole show, including the repertoire, Luciano Pavarotti said that Cameroon was going to win the Cup. I did not agree, although I conceded that Cameroon had very good players. Luciano bet me, in front of everybody, one hundred dollars, reiterating his conviction. I thought immediately that from a mathematical point of view it was an easy bet for me; Cameroon against all the other teams. The probabilities favored me tremendously, so I accepted the challenge—and we had many witnesses! We met once again in New York and another time in Barcelona.

Finally, back in L.A., I started to write the new program, which included two medleys. Suddenly I received word that many Hollywood celebrities were going to attend the concert, including Frank Sinatra, so the tenors decided to render a tribute to Mario Lanza in deference to the film industry. The production office faxed me two lead sheets of songs that had been performed by Lanza, "Because" and "Because I Love You." Only one had been chosen, but I did not know which one. Tibor Rudas was also confused. I knew that Domingo and Carreras were in Europe, but it was 5:00 p.m. in Los Angeles (2:00 a.m. on the Continent), and I could not wake them up. I took a chance and called Pavarotti at his residence in New York (8:00 p.m.). He answered the phone and I told him my predicament. I said, "If you sing the first bars I shall know which song I must orchestrate." He started to sing "Because" and kept going, continuing on with a second and third chorus with a lot of enthusiasm and gusto. I was speechless, and when he finally finished I said, "You know, I had Luciano Pavarotti singing for me, alone!" His response was, "Yes, but it is going to cost you." Immediately I answered, "No, it won't cost me anything, remember Cameroon? We are even now."

The concert was another success, but I had a disagreeable experience. My credits were not included in the telecast, and my attorney brought a lawsuit against Tibor Rudas for damages. This was an unnecessary waste of time and energy, but many people around the world knew about my participation in the event, and I felt embarrassed and disappointed. Finally we went to court, and the settlement was largely in my favor. As my wife, my attorney, and I were walking through the parking lot to get in the car and go celebrate our victory, Tibor Rudas's second in command was following us. Actually, nothing happened because he was only doing the same thing, trying to get to his car. At dinner I said, "Rudas will call me again!" Donna and my attorney thought that I had lost my mind. Tibor Rudas was known to have a big ego and actually had reasons to feel so superior because he was a very successful businessman and had enjoyed a great many triumphs thanks to his imagination and boldness.

Since the next World Cup was going to take place in France, the 1988 concert was planned to be performed at the Eiffel Tower. The phone rang and Rudas was on the line. He said, "This is a difficult call for me to make, but the 'boys' [meaning the tenors] like you." So we made peace, and this time he made sure that the credits, publicity, and public relations were going to be covered as far as I was concerned. He invited me to the press conference in Paris, where pictures were taken of me playing soccer with the three tenors.

The final concert in 2002 took place in Osaka since the World Cup was being played in Japan and Korea. This time the producer was Tadao Terajima. He is a true gentleman. Our contract was easy to fulfill, and there were no problems. The Osaka event was the last of the Three Tenors concerts. And as I listen and watch the Osaka video, their voices are vibrating in the particles of time in which I've immersed myself with the opera candelabra, the echoes of Puccini, Verdi, and the obligatory Neapolitan songs and encores.

Notes

1. In mitigation, it should be said that Teotihucan is isolated and that the Spanish convent was the closest convenient place for such a celebration.

2. Jose Carreras ended up singing my "Granada" arrangement, which Placido Domingo graciously offered to him.

3. Just as the screenwriter for *The Sting* had to make sure that Paul Newman had as many lines as Robert Redford.

4. Was this his idea of "Esperanto"?

~

CHAPTER TWENTY-NINE

A Polynesian Adventure— *Lili' Uokalani Symphony*

The roots of another of my musical/spiritual experiences have almost biblical connotations. The Polynesian people are the inhabitants of a group of islands in the South Pacific, whose total land arc is 225,000 square kilometers. The main islands are Samoa, Tonga, Fiji, Easter Island, Tahiti, and other groups in Western Polynesia, including parts of New Zealand. More than two thousand years ago, the inhabitants of these islands, dispersed within 30,000,000 square kilometers of ocean and having no means of communication among themselves, had what amounts to a mystical calling: they all felt, at the same time, that a promised land was waiting for them and decided to make the journey to find it. From different directions they took their primitive canoes and confronted the elements. Many of them died during this exodus, castigated by fiery storms, but others landed temporarily on the west coast of Mexico, where they met the Aztec tribes moving south. Finally, the survivors of this awesome migration arrived at their promised land destination, which happened to be the then-unpopulated Hawaiian Islands. This is why the original inhabitants of Hawaii and their language and customs are Polynesian.

Without knowing anything much of this amazing history, I had visited the different Hawaiian Islands for more than thirty years. My vacations with my wife and children allowed me to relax, swim, explore, read (not books about music), and enjoy the different cuisines available and offered by the great chefs of China, Thailand, Japan, and Europe. However, even during these vacations I was practicing piano at least one hour a day, and in order to avoid the press and other intrusions I registered in the hotels under the name of Glenn Cockrell. Glenn is in the oil business; he is also my brother-in-law and, like my wife, from Oklahoma. One afternoon, while practicing at the hotel's bar, I noticed an older couple listening to some Chopin and Bach I was playing. They came to me and asked, "What is your name?" "Glenn Cockrell," I answered. "Oh, we've heard a lot about you. You are very famous!"

Gradually, people found out about my visits to this wonderful place, and eventually Donald Johanos, who was the music director of the Honolulu Symphony, contacted me and thereafter invited me frequently to guest conduct. The local jazz disc jockey invited me to be interviewed on his program, and I also started to participate in the Honolulu International Jazz Festival, which invited musicians from the Pacific Rim to perform in the company of some good local players.

One day, Donald Johanos organized a luncheon with an attorney for the Lili'Uokalani Foundation, Mr. Neil Hannas, and his music adviser, Mr. Aaron Mahi. They had heard the *Cantos Aztecas* CD and felt that I had the sensitivity to understand the music of multicultural streams. Since the only thing I knew about Hawaiian music was the ukulele, I listened very carefully to their conversation. They talked about the last queen of Hawaii, Lili'Uokalani, and wanted to commission me to write a symphony in her memory, which would be premiered by Donald Johanos and his orchestra.

Lili'Uokalani was an extraordinary lady. As a queen, in the middle of a patriarchal Victorian society, she understood that only through education could women in Hawaii achieve financial independence, dignity, and respect; she was also a composer. I became intrigued by their proposal, and they provided a lot of material about her—a biography, the history of Hawaii, and the traditions of the Polynesian people—and the possibility of writing a composition in which ethnic elements would be combined with a universal musical language attracted me very much: the results might encapsulate the Queen's spirit, endurance, and strength.

I decided the work should be a long one, rather like a mural, because there was a lot to tell and the project demanded large-scale thematic expositions, developments, and variations. My first decision was to avoid the Hawaiian and Pan-Pacific pop music: I needed to go to the Polynesian roots. Also, I had heard in my mind the imposing presence of volcanoes, which featured prominently in their mythology. But I needed help and further research in order to organize the building blocks of such an ambitious project, particularly in terms of a metaphor I wanted to create in the second movement of the symphony, in which the Queen is under arrest and the bird is in a cage singing its sad song. At the same time, an eight-note melody began to haunt me. I became obsessed with it, and while in my studio in Los Angeles, I was impelled to write it down on sketch paper with the purpose of incorporating it somewhere into the composition. With both things in mind, I asked the Department of Ornithology from the University of Hawaii to send me sample recordings of their native birdsongs.[1] They sent me more than one hundred samples, from which I chose a particularly beautiful and unusual one voiced by the *oo'aa* bird.

An extraordinary coincidence happened when I returned to Honolulu. First, the conservator of the royal palace showed me the rooms where the Queen had been under arrest after she was deposed by the Americans and the British. She had, on the balcony, many *oo'aas* in cages and discovered that they died in captivity![2] I was then told that, according to tradition, each Hawaiian monarch had his or her own bell calls that rang from the church across from the palace; these consisted of different combinations of eight notes. I went to the church's campanile where eight people played the bells: Lili'Uokalani's permutation formed exactly the haunting melody that was in my mind for several weeks!

Were these mere coincidences or paranormal phenomena? I was totally bewildered. Carl Jung has studied the aspects of chance, coincidence, and cause and effect. His conclusion is that there is a synchronicity in time, which could explain this kind of phenomenon. He ends his essay on the *I Ching* (the Chinese book of changes, which is an oracle based on chance). "The *I Ching* is for the benefit of those who can discern its meaning." My own attitude was to take advantage of these messages, perhaps from the Polynesian gods, and continue my work.

The *Lili'Uokalani Symphony* was premiered in Honolulu under Donald Johanos's baton. The performance brought the Hawaiian audience to tears, and great emotion overtook me. I knew these intense inspirations did not always possess me; perhaps it is a blessing. There is an energy in the Universe, and it is possible that we can all tap into it sometimes.

The Lili'Uokalani Foundation sponsored the recording of the work with the Vienna Symphony, this time under my baton. A recording engineer was brought from Salzburg, and the sessions took place in a theater instead of in a studio. After the recording, Aaron Mahi sang for the Austrian musicians a Polynesian chant.

Notes

1. I had learned from the great Olivier Messiaen how to translate birdsongs to the human ear.

2. Unsurprisingly, the *oo'aa* is now extinct.

CHAPTER THIRTY

~

The Paris Philharmonic

Jean-Claude Dubois is a very influential figure in the Parisian music circles. On a prior visit to the French capital, while I was recording the music for another movie, he and a group of musicians and businessmen and women came to me with a proposal that I become the music director of the Paris Philharmonic Orchestra. I couldn't believe it, but I accepted. Donna and I started to look for apartments to stay in while the rehearsals and concerts were taking place. But the board of directors decided that was not necessary: they would take care of the hotel expenses. So yet another new adventure began.

I already had experience as a music director of the Glendale Symphony Orchestra in Los Angeles. Then and now, the post involved not only conducting but also designing the programming and hiring guest artists and conductors to lead the orchestra when I was unable to be in France. I worked with them for two years, and we gave good concerts. But when I realized that my job involved not only music but fund-raising as well, I started to feel impatient and slowly made the decision to quit. Ali Khan (Aga Khan's son) was a big supporter, but the luncheons with him in his private club were so long that I barely had time to study scores. And in the afternoons and evenings, Le Tout Paris kept Donna and I very busy with their high teas, dinner parties, and all kinds of receptions, which made my life very difficult. After all, I am not only a conductor but a composer as well. And although I had a lot of fun and we made much fine music, after two years I took a sabbatical, and then I resigned.

CHAPTER THIRTY-ONE

Bix

Leon Bismarck "Bix" Beiderbecke was an extremely gifted cornet and trumpet player. He came from a German émigré family who established themselves in Davenport, Iowa. His father was in the lumber business and expected his son to follow in his footsteps; however, from an early age, Bix showed an unusual inclination for music and decided to find his own destiny. He became the first to record the famous trumpet solo from *Concerto in F* by George Gershwin, who was present during the session as Bix's friend.

Louis Armstrong was Bix's idol, and he waited for the boat coming up the Mississippi River where he could play duets with his master; Armstrong called him "my boy." Unfortunately, in those days there were of course segregation laws, and black and white musicians were not allowed to play together. Surrounded by rather mediocre players, Bix did his best to express his musical ideas. The sound of his cornet shone in the middle of the bands and ensembles around him. His solos were fresh and innovative, his tone rather introverted and with a touch of melancholy even during the most joyful of tunes. He also became a composer of piano pieces, such as "In a Mist," which was very much influenced by Debussy.

But his frustration, the lack of understanding (even from own family), and a self-destructive search for perfection he knew he couldn't achieve led to depression and alcoholism. He died in 1931 when he was barely twenty-eight years old.

In 1997, the members of the Bix Beiderbecke Jazz Memorial Society approached me. They had heard my recording of *Jazz Meets the Symphony* and wanted me to write a composition in his honor. I was invited to Davenport, Iowa, and they took me to the cemetery to visit his grave: I felt that even if his remains were there, his energy was somewhere else. Then they showed me the house where he was born, which had been bought by an Italian film director, Pupi Avati, whom I had met at the Cannes Film Festival the previous year (where we were co-jurors at the festival) and who made a movie called *Bix*. The house, which had been condemned, became his office, and with the help of Mr. Douglas Miller (whom I also met in Cannes), he remodeled it and saved it from destruction.

The next step in my tour by the members of the Memorial Society was a visit to the Davenport Museum where, in a rather small room, Bix Beiderbecke's piano was on display. My first reaction was respectful, but I must confess that it left me rather indifferent. They were all waiting for me to sit down at the instrument and play something, which I was not prepared for. At that point in my life, my repertoire was quite different from what they were almost certainly expecting from me: moreover, I had not heard a Bix recording since I was fourteen years old—about fifty years earlier! Silence, suspense, and indecision faced me at the piano. My hands were not moving; my fingers didn't know what to do.

Suddenly, a miracle. The tunes that Bix used to play, like "Royal Garden Blues," "At the Jazz Band Ball," and "Davenport Blues," flooded back into my memory. Not only that: I could hear him playing, his particular sound, his phrasing, even his interruptions to take a breath. And I started to accompany him! This sounds crazy, but all the people in the room felt the same thing; and extraordinary emotions came out of our memories into our hearts, to be translated into chills that overcame each one of us. Afterward, we were speechless. I had not played any melody; I did not show off my command of the instrument, no arpeggios, no ornaments, just simple accompaniment in the style of the Wolverines, which was Bix's band. At that moment I decided to write *Rhapsody for Bix*, and my desire to memorialize him developed into a composition that interweaved his music, his love for Debussy, his proximity to the Mississippi River, the "speak-easy" atmospheres of Chicago where he spent a great part of his short life, and my own original theme.

The world premiere took place later that year in a new auditorium, and twelve thousand people attended. James Morrison played Bix's cornet that evening, while the drummer was Louis Bellson, who was born across the Mississippi River in Moulin, Illinois. The bass player, Dave Carpenter, was from Los Angeles, and the Davenport Symphony Orchestra completed the rest of the cast. It was not only a success with the public and the members of the

Memorial Society, but also brought the satisfaction of having solved an artistic problem through love and memories.[1]

Note

1. *Rhapsody for Bix* was recorded for Aleph Records in 1998 with James Morrison, Ray Brown, Jeff Hamilton, and the London Symphony Orchestra.

CHAPTER THIRTY-TWO

~

Oman

At the end of 1999, Zubin Mehta, in Los Angeles for a concert with the Israel Philharmonic, told me that the Sultan of Oman—a lover of classical music and indeed a classmate of Zubin's in Bombay during his early studies—had contacted him through his chief of staff. The Sultan wished to find a composer to write a symphonic piece based on the traditional music of Oman; Maestro Mehta recommended me and suggested that if I had the inclination and the time I should do it. "Do they know that although you are not Jewish, you are the music director of the Israel Philharmonic Orchestra?" I asked him. He answered, "Don't worry about it!"

A week later, I received a fax from Oman inviting me to visit the country for meetings about the project at the end of March 2000. Although I was familiar with Arab music, I didn't know too much about the music of this particular country. Fate—and previous conducting contracts—dictated that my journey start in Reykjavik, Iceland, at the end of February and then continue through France and Germany before my final destination, Oman. I took two suitcases, one with winter clothes, the other with summer ones.

The weather in Iceland was extremely cruel. My hotel was across the street from the concert hall, but it was almost impossible to negotiate the slippery ice and melting snow. Conditions eased as I went south, and after the last European concert I flew from Frankfurt to Oman. However, the airplane had to stop to refuel in Kuwait, and I got a little nervous there, thinking that eight years earlier Saddam Hussein's army had invaded the place. But late the same evening I arrived in Muscat, Oman's capital, without incident—except

161

that one of my suitcases had been lost. The one containing my summer clothes, naturally.

Nevertheless, I was excited to be in a part of the world I had never explored before. During the ride to the hotel I was awed by the peculiar landscape and the architecture of the beautiful homes in which traditional and modern styles converged, and the Al Bustan Palace turned out to be one of the most remarkable hotels in which I have ever stayed. The sense of space, the sculptured walls, the immense cupola, and the sumptuous lobbies, corridors, and suites, which were perfumed by continuously burning incense, made me definitively aware that I was in the Orient. Where would my musical adventures take me next?

The following day, after buying some suitable clothes, I was driven to an official building where I met the Minister of Information, Abdulaziz Al Roa, and his chief of staff, Salim Almahruqui. We talked about their civilization, which is not alien to me. The etymology of my first language, Spanish, is 80% Latin and 20% Arabic. The Moors (Arabs) had occupied the Iberian Peninsula for eight centuries. One of their most prominent philosophers was Averroes, who was born in Spain. We also talked about the fact that while Europe was submerged in the Middle (dark) Ages, the Islamic civilization was flourishing. The Arabs saved the manuscripts of the Greek thinkers, which they were convinced would be destroyed by the intolerant Christian warlords; miraculously, they were taken to the Library of Alexandria. There is also a great deal of Platonic and Aristotelian influence in Islamic culture.

We then proceeded to discuss the purpose of my visit: the symphonic work based on Oman's traditional music. A musicologist brought me a great number of books, records, videotapes, and cassettes containing information about the nation's songs, dances, and instrumental music. Since I could not take everything with me, they promised to send this monumental material to my address in Los Angeles. I told them that I would study it all and then let them know whether I could commit to such a serious project. Then I was taken on a tour of the city, which made me think of the legend of the 1,001 Arabian Nights. We visited the Bazaar, the Portuguese forts, the Sultan's Palace, and the old city, and I felt that fantasy and reality were pages of the same book.

Back in Los Angeles, I awaited the package with a mixture of anticipation and anxiety; however, when it arrived a week later, my first reaction was disappointment. The Omani melodies are very short and keep repeating ad infinitum; furthermore, there is no development, no contrasting motifs. Their rhythms, on the other hand, introduced by African slaves (like jazz), are extremely sophisticated and complex.

I decided to solve the problem by using their themes as an accompaniment to the rhythmic structure, rather than as the main melodic strains, and adding my own themes and harmonies as the vertebral column—a method that would further enhance the orchestral colors, which was the fundamental *raison d'être* of the piece. One of the points we all agreed on was to avoid the use of ethnic instruments, but like a painter, I would be able to evoke them with orchestral devices and combinations. Invigorated by these ideas and schemes, I accepted the challenge; my patrons got very excited and invited me to attend a festival of Omani music, which was going to take place in Muscat at the beginning of 2001.

Writing this score reminded me more forcibly than on most other occasions of Igor Stravinsky's observation that the work of a composer is similar to that of a shoemaker: you get the shape of the shoe after a lot of physical and mental effort. Even so, I was halfway finished by the time I went back to Oman in February 2001. But there were clouds on the horizon. The head of the Al-Qaeda terrorist organization, Bin Laden, had given an order to kill any Americans, anywhere—and I was traveling in a particularly incendiary part of the world. Fortunately, according to Argentinean law, once born in Argentina one is always an Argentine citizen and has an Argentine passport. Besides, having been appointed honorary cultural adviser to the president of Argentina, I also had a diplomatic passport.

As a matter of fact, a few years before, a Spanish film producer wanted to hire me to write the score of the film *Don Quixote*, but I had to be a Spanish citizen to be able to work on it because there were already many foreigners involved in the pre-production and principal photography. Emiliano Piedra found a loophole in the laws of his country. Apparently, Spain did not fully recognize Argentinean independence. Therefore, I was still a Spanish citizen (perhaps by extension, a member of the European Union?).

The connection of this subplot to the Omani saga is that Cervantes, who wrote *Don Quixote*, attributed it to a fictional Arab writer, Cide Hamete Benengeli. In the introduction to his classical work, Cervantes claims he found the very book he was writing in the Arab section of a bookstore in Toledo! In any event, it did cross my mind during the flight that since I was the only Westerner on the plane, those Argentinean passports could well save my life; as things turned out, I reached Muscat with no alarms.

His Excellency, Abdulaziz Al Roa, invited me to dinner at his home.[1] Mr. Al Roas is a collector of Islamic art but also appreciates art from the West; he commissioned an American painter to create pictures based on Omani history and legends. As a matter of fact, it was revealed to me during the visit to the art gallery that the tale of Sinbad the Sailor was Omani. Later, an English explorer, Tim Severin, recreated the seven voyages of Sinbad. Using a replica of a medieval Arabian ship made from Malabar timber held together with coconut ropes with a crew that included Omanis, he sailed from the port of Sohar to China to investigate the adventures of the sea-faring hero.

During this second visit to Oman, I attended a music festival where thousands of spectators enjoyed the music and the dances. I also met some of the musicians, who showed and played for me the ethnic instruments. All this helped me to have faith in the possibility of an understanding between the different cultures. After all, we all belong to the human race, and music (Esperanto) helps to bridge and unite through its universal form of communication. But the events of September 11, 2001, unfortunately prove that mankind has not yet learned the lesson that intolerance and fanaticism are plagues that need to be eliminated if we want to co-exist or indeed survive on this planet.

The *Symphonic Impressions of Oman* was recorded at the Abbey Road Studios by the London Symphony Orchestra under my baton. While I was returning to the hotel, I couldn't help but remember the lines written by the Arab philosopher Averroes: "The Children's melodies across the Guadalquivir are the voices of light, the sounds of love."

Note

1. Actually, "home" isn't quite right: it was a veritable mansion, boasting an architecture and an interior decoration whose sense of space is utterly different from Western styles. For a while when I returned, I found my large and comfortable studio too crowded in comparison.

PART VII

DONNA

CHAPTER THIRTY-THREE

~

Romanza: For Donna

In 1969, Dr. Walter Rubsamen, who was the head of the University of California's (Los Angeles) music department, asked me to teach composition at his institution.

"I am grateful for your offer," I said, "but I have no experience and no teaching methodology."

"Don't worry, just put pressure on them," he responded.

I accepted this new challenge but on three conditions. Since I was very busy, the classes would have to take place on Thursdays; there was to be a maximum of twelve students; and each one would be auditioned first.

Most of the resultant group were trained in twentieth-century classical techniques; some of them had jazz roots; and there were two who could express their ideas only through the use of electronic instruments. I enjoyed communicating with these young people, especially as it was a two-way process: they were willing to learn from the thoughts I shared with them, but in turn I learned things from their questions. A nice relationship developed between us, and I invited them to the recording sessions of the films I was scoring at the time.

But something different that was going to change my life completely also took place on Thursday afternoons at UCLA. Every week at the end of class, as I was going from Schoenberg Hall (the music department) to my car, I saw a beautiful lady walking in the direction of the main library. Her beauty was unusual—long hair, refined features on her face, very intense eyes, and a distinctive silhouette. Every Thursday I would recognize her undulating figure.

I was going through a divorce from my first wife, but I did not dare to approach this woman who started to walk into my dreams. In those days, I was living and working in a house close to my children's residence. Besides my work, on weekends I was taking them to parks—Disneyland, San Diego, San Francisco, and so on. But more than ever I was immersing myself in my work. The visits with my children, the sporadic social activity, and waiting for Thursday afternoons at UCLA were like an ocean in which I was floating without a sense of real personal direction.

However, I had a group of friends and landed at parties given by Bronislau Kaper, who composed "Green Dolphin Street" among many other songs and film scores.[1] Kaper was born in Poland, and every time Arthur Rubinstein came to Los Angeles he stayed in his home and practiced on his Steinway. The gatherings used to take place in the afternoons, and we all ended up going to some restaurant, continuing our endless conversations, storytelling, and jokes.

And then I received an invitation from some Argentinean friends to a dinner party that was going to take place in the house of an American lady and her Peruvian girlfriend. An Argentinean filmmaker and other South American friends were going to attend, and my first reaction was to accept. But as the days were going by, I started to have doubts. With a few exceptions, I didn't really know anybody who was going to be there, and I was reluctant to make small talk and superficial comments about the weather or the zodiac. Even so, I did tell my cook that the following Friday she could leave early.

But when Friday arrived, my indecision cleared; I would cancel and eat alone in a nearby restaurant. I phoned the house, not even knowing the name of the lady who was giving the party! A very seductive voice answered, and her "Hello" immediately changed my mind. I asked, "Who is this?" "My name is Donna," the voice answered. That was enough to prompt me to make a 180-degree turn: I gave her my name right away and confirmed that I was looking forward to coming and asked her at what time the party started (a good recovery from my initial plan!).

When that Friday evening arrived, I drove to her place. I rang the doorbell . . . and could not believe what happened next! The UCLA lady whom I thought was a dream opened the door. Here she was, facing me, smiling, and welcoming me! I knew it was she; I remembered vividly her figure, her face, her long hair, and her beauty as well as her interesting features. She told me later that she felt a mutual recognition although she had never met me before.

I stayed after the dinner until 2:00 in the morning. A few recalcitrant guests also stayed and were chatting and drinking wine and enjoying their stay. But Donna and I took advantage of their indifference: attracted to each other, we started to exchange ideas in one of the most fateful dialogues of my life. I noticed some interesting paintings on her walls; she told me they were hers. Her talent, intelligence, and sensitivity were also a part of my feelings for her. To be sure, she was "Thursday afternoons" on the university campus: she confirmed that she was getting her master's degree in English literature, and at exactly the same time as I was leaving Schoenberg Hall, she would be passing by on the way to the UCLA main library.

As I was leaving her house, I invited her to a concert in which I was performing the following week with the Los Angeles Philharmonic at the Music Center. Donna told me later that it was not usual for her to be accompanied by a man in tails, in front of an orchestra, on a first date. And this is the way our relationship started; we even joked about improving Argentinean-Oklahoma relations.

The irony is that two weeks before I met Donna, my mother, who had been visiting me, told me at the Los Angeles airport, ready to return to Buenos Aires, "Son, I see that you are busy, that you have friends, and that your career is going well, but your loneliness disquiets me." "Don't worry, Mother, I am all right. One thing you can be sure of is that I'll never remarry." Famous last words . . .

Six months later, on the 1st of August, 1971, the wedding took place between Donna and me. We shared joy and companionship; we exchanged ideas; sometimes I was afraid that we thought so much alike that perhaps our dialogues would become soliloquies! She shared her favorite authors with me, while I made her aware of the new developments in Latin American literature.

When my first wife passed away, Donna adopted my two children from that marriage: William, born in New York City in 1960, who is now a screenplay writer, and Francis, born in Los Angeles in 1967, now a graphic artist. Donna and I have a son, Ryan, who was born in 1973 and is a film director as well as a screenwriter. Donna raised the three kids and supervised their education very closely. I encouraged her to improve her artistic techniques, and she took classes with a Russian master, Sergei Bongard. Her paintings are masterpieces, and she has received offers to have them exhibited in prestigious galleries, but she has refused to do so, perhaps because of her high standards and intense self-criticism. I respect her reasons, although I do not understand them.

We also traveled together and enjoyed business trips as well as vacations. She took to many of my old friends, like Henry Mancini, Ray Brown, Zubin Mehta, and their wives; we also of course made new friends. As my career diversified, she started to abandon her art lessons and became more involved in my business, supervising the attorneys, accountants, agents, and managers working for me. She read all the contracts, which underwent a metamorphosis during my professional engagements. The written agreements used to be one page; now they are as thick as a telephone book.

But above all we are partners, lovers, and friends, sharing an unusual happiness that has lasted thirty-six years so far and keeps going on. Sometimes we would like to freeze time, not for the obvious fear of the aging process, but rather to prolong our companionship.

I shall always remember our visit to Claude Monet's museum in Giverny as a symbol of the parallel of the color of Donna's eyes with the gardens that the great French master composed for his paintings. The sun inundated the universe with a rain of light, colors, and love.

Note

1. Among his friends were Henry Miller, Zubin Mehta, and the Polish painter Witold-K, who miraculously preserved his life by not going to Sharon Tate's house that tragic night when the serial killer Charles Manson and his followers committed their infamous murders.

PART VIII

FINALE

CHAPTER THIRTY-FOUR

~

Things to Come

In 1998, the Los Angeles Music Center gave the Distinguished Artist Awards to some of those who made an outstanding contribution to the arts. I was one of the recipients and attended the event. Kirk Douglas, who was honored after me, said, "Lalo Schifrin and I worked together on a film many years ago [*The Brotherhood*]. I am practically retired, but Lalo keeps going on, and on, and on!" The next day, a car picked me up to take me to a television interview. I noticed that the driver was very old, but in great physical and mental shape. I asked him what his secret was and he said, "Slow down!"

Is it possible that the key to explaining my multiple activities and the vigor with which I have dedicated a life to music is this: that the child in Buenos Aires who was eager to learn, curious about how sounds are juxtaposed, intrigued by nonverbal communication between the conductor and orchestra, mesmerized by the operatic drama within the play of life and the celebration after conquering the difficulties in every battle with the piano, is still within me? The spirit of that child who was hypnotized by the movies and later on fell in love with jazz, painting, literature is still living—on, on, on. As long as the feeling of wonder does not abandon me, as long as I can hear the sounds of the sunrise and smell the perfumes of my dreams, I'll keep going on and on. But I need to feel that the energy of the universe, which we call God, will keep flowing through my veins. That energy has helped me so far, and as long as I have something to say, I'll keep on writing and performing.

In *The Garden of the Forking Paths*, Borges speculates on the choices we are offered. And in music, the choices are infinite: the possibilities of sound combinations with the acoustic instruments of a symphony orchestra, a jazz band, or a chamber ensemble have not yet been exhausted. What has been done in the field of electronic music so far has not even scratched the surface of a vast continent to be explored. From the past we have received a heritage that keeps expanding. The so-called ethnic music, the sounds of voices and instruments from all the cultures, can and should be incorporated.

Science teaches us that there is a difference between a physical mixture, where the components can be separated and returned to their original state, and the chemical combination, in which a new element is created, perhaps after a dramatic combustion. Ludwig Von Beethoven was fascinated by the music of the gypsies during the Austro-Hungarian Empire and incorporated it into his own work, as in the last movement of his Seventh Symphony. For myself, I would like to include rock music: some of the Beatles' songs; Emerson, Lake & Palmer; and Tangerine Dream have given us examples that pop music can be good and stimulating. Also, the sampling methods of rap artists' music can be incorporated and even expanded to new dimensions for all of us who can move like chameleons between different musical languages.

At the Paris Conservatory, we used to make fun of some of the Olivier Messiaen's ideas. He had studied and elaborated a methodology of birdsongs; he was also a mystic Catholic who echoed Bach in saying, "I write for the glory of God."[1] Our joke was "Let's write the ornithology of angels to please him!" But in view of all the landscapes that we could explore, this is not really a joke anymore. We can make the angels sing while making a bell's overtones merge with Hindu sitars or making a working jazz rhythm section the foundation of an eighteenth-century English consort in which the sounds are transformed by electronic means. With the means of communications we have now, why not take advantage of the universal kaleidoscope of sounds?

During one of my visits to the Louvre Museum, I found in an almost forgotten corner a collection of Persian miniatures. It was an extraordinary archeological treasure and each one of the diminutive statues a true work of art, very sophisticated and moving. I couldn't help but wonder if jazz was going to end in the same forgotten corner of our collective memory; it was at that moment that I vowed to devote my energies and time to the fight for my beloved art form, not just to be remembered but to assist its growth by contributing its own innovations. Like the fate of some of the eternal punishment inflicted upon the heroes in Greek mythology, we travel on our own journeys toward our horizons only to find, when we arrive, that there is another one, and then another one, and so on *ad infinitum*. Even if I am condemned to suffer Sisyphus's fate, I feel that my conviction will help me to face the difficulties. And my resolution is already invigorated by the exam-

ple of other artists who felt energized by the wonders of cross-fertilization—
Stravinsky's *Ragtime*, Darius Milhaud's *La Création du Monde*, and Hans
Werner Henze's Third Symphony being just three notable examples.

A literary example is furnished by the Cuban writer Alejo Carpentier, the
author of a novel titled *Concerto Barroco*. The narrative takes place in the
eighteenth century during the Spanish colonization of Mexico. A wealthy
lord, a music lover and aficionado who collects manuscripts of the great composers of his time, decides to embark on a journey with his black servant and
confidant to Italy in order to meet Antonio Vivaldi and ask the maestro for
some of his manuscripts. After a long journey with many incidents and adventures, his wishes are at last fulfilled. But, after meeting Vivaldi and attending one of his rehearsals, the music of Louis Armstrong is revealed to
him: an energetic rendition of "I Can't Give You Anything but Love, Baby"
with brilliant improvisations by Satchmo.

That is of course an anachronism, but perhaps the universe is an anachronism. Walt Whitman said, "The clock marks the hour but what marks eternity?" In modern physics, beyond relativity and quanta, there are theories
about nine or ten dimensions of space and two of time. It is possible that particles of time are flowing from the future. My nephew David, who is an as-
trophysicist and works for NASA, told me, "It will not be impossible to build
a time machine, although it will be very expensive." I said that if that happens, we would already know about it.

David: Why?

Me: Because people from the future would already be among us.

David: How do you know that they are not here?

Ever since I was a composition student, I have felt that time in music
could flow backwards. It is proven in the canons by contrary motion, and if
one concentrates with intensity, one can feel this second dimension of time.

But what about the *powers* of music, and also of the movies?

The French poet Baudelaire wrote in a piece entitled *Correspondences* that
"the perfumes, the colors and the sounds correspond to each other like infinite
shadows that sing the transports of the spirit and the senses." Olivier Messiaen
conceived a scale of notes from the diatonic scale and colors from the rainbow;
he even wrote a work titled *Chronocromie* in which he added the sense of time
to these correspondences. Since the late twentieth century, many artists have
gotten together to create audiovisual works, and there are expos and museums
around the world that take advantage of these collaborations, even if in many

cases the result is so far less than satisfactory. And films, which became the opera of our time, reflect better than any other art form the correspondence between literature, theater, visual arts, and music, and they touch a nerve with the masses to the point that it has become arguably our most popular art form.

Another path in this Borgean garden leads us to the matter of perception. The history of music is the history of perception, first by composers and then by the public, of the new sounds (harmonics) that are triggered by a fundamental tone. The reader may try an experiment in front of a church. Listen to the bells, and keep searching for the overtones that keep accruing until they slowly evanesce and disappear. In one hundred years, the history of jazz has mirrored the evolution of two thousand years of European music: the early monody corresponds with the blues shouts on the plantation, the polyphony in the Renaissance with the New Orleans and Dixieland bands, the romantic era (which needed the expression of a symphony orchestra and more sophisticated harmonies) with the Big Band era, and finally, the dissolution of tonality with modern and free jazz.

The better one can hear the most distant overtones of the bell, the more equipped one is to perceive the music of our time. And there is another dimension to this aspect of perception: music is an art that happens not only in time but also in space—there is a *distance* between sounds that we should be able to perceive. Of course, the easiest one is horizontal, silence that separates two or more musical fragments. The romantics knew how to use silence as a dramatic tool, like the beginning of Beethoven's Fifth Symphony. But there is also a distance between simultaneous sounds. If we can perceive how that distance opens and closes we may enjoy a richer musical and aesthetic experience.

As a matter of fact, in the old Chinese civilization the musicians did not have names for the individual notes of their scales, but they established a nomenclature for the intervals (distances) between the notes. The next step is to be able to listen to the other side of the sounds. This idea came to me once when I walked backstage at Carnegie Hall and Charles Mingus's band was performing. Their music, which I already knew, became another entity from that perspective, like walking on the other side of the moon.

All these concepts, and many more, could be construed as an abstract speculation unless they have a human face. When my father died in Buenos Aires in 1979, I was unable to attend the services because I was under a death threat from one of the many military dictatorships that my country has been condemned to suffer. And in July of 1997, while I was playing a piano recital at the Castle of Elmau in the Bavarian Alps, I received the news that my mother passed away from a stroke. It takes two hours to drive to Munich, and by the time all the flight connections could be made (Munich, Frankfort, Rio de Janeiro, Buenos Aires), I had arrived too late for her funeral.

Homer said that the gods have given us misfortune so that we can sing. But the same gods have given us joy, a sense of humor, and especially, the capacity to appreciate the aesthetic pleasure of making, participating in, and sharing our songs. Mankind needs to sing, and the gods have given us the possibility to be creative and innovative, along with the imagination to plumb our infinite musical thoughts. We composers, like all creative artists, receive messages from those gods; we need to have the tools to take dictation and also to elaborate our own extensions of those messages.

I do not think that the time machine is going to be invented in order for me to say, musically, everything I need to say. And that is the real *Mission: Impossible*. It is true that all the awards, medals, accolades, and recognitions for my accomplishments are great ego stimulators. But they are also very dangerous. I knew a composer in Hollywood who, once he won an Oscar, stopped writing. His soul started to die before his body did.

The Italian producer Dino de Laurentiis wanted to hear Igor Stravinsky write the score for the film *The Bible*. Obviously, he was thinking how appropriate the introduction to *The Rite of Spring* would be to the mood of *Genesis*. Stravinsky asked for several million dollars as a fee. De Laurentiis asked, "If I pay you that amount, do you know how much it is going to cost me?" The composer replied, "It will cost me more!"

As I am growing old, my memories keep accumulating. But I keep my dreams as alive as when I was young. This symmetry forces me to ask for Borges's help to find the right coda to this labyrinth of mirrors, which has been my life in music so far.

After many years, I have observed that beauty, like happiness, is frequent.

There is no one day in which for one instant we are not in Paradise.

—Jorge Luis Borges, *The Conspirator*, 1983

And to that I will add a wonderful remark by Friedrich Nietzsche that goes to the heart of what I believe and have experienced:

Without music, life would be a mistake.

Note

1. In Messiaen's case, Christ from the Roman Catholic apostolic dogma.

~

Appendix: Composer Credits

Feature Films

2007	Rush Hour 3	New Line Cinema
2006	Abominable	Red Circle Productions
2004	After the Sunset	New Line Cinema
2004	The Bridge of San Luis Rey	British Films
2002	Bringing Down the House	Walt Disney Productions
2001	Rush Hour 2: Remember the Dragon	New Line Cinema
1999	Jack of All Trades	Pearl Cam Productions
1998	Rush Hour	New Line Cinema
1998	Something to Believe In	Lord Lew Grade Productions
1998	Tango (a Carlos Saura Film)	Pandora Cinema
1997	Money Talks	New Line Cinema
1996	Mission: Impossible (original theme)	Paramount
1995	Rice, Beans and Ketchup	Beco Films, Inc.
1995	Scorpion Spring	New Line Cinema
1993	The Beverly Hillbillies	Fox
1992	FX 2: The Deadly Art of Illusion	Dodi Fayed-Jack Wiener
1991	Naked Tango	Gotan
1989	Fridays of Eternity	Aries Productions
1989	Return to the River Kwai	Columbia Pictures
1988	Berlin Blues	Cannon Film Distributors
1988	The Dead Pool	Warner Bros.

1988	Little Sweetheart	BBC Productions
1988	The Silence at Bethany	PBS
1987	The Fourth Protocol	Fourth Protocol
1986	Bad Medicine	Fox
1986	Black Moon Rising	New World Pictures
1986	The Ladies Club	Media Home Entertainment
1986	Mean Season	United Artists
1986	The New Kids	Columbia Pictures
1984	Tank	Lorimar
1983	Doctor Detroit	Universal
1983	The Osterman Weekend	Columbia Pictures
1983	*The Sting II	Universal
1983	Sudden Impact	Warner Bros.
1982	Amityville II: The Possession	Dino De Laurentiis
1982	The Class of 1984	Guerilla High Productions
1982	Fast-Walking	MGM
1982	Los Viernes de la Eternidad	Aries Productions
1982	A Stranger Is Watching	MGM
1981	Buddy, Buddy	MGM
1981	Caveman	United Artists
1981	Loophole	Brent Walker
1981	La Pelle/The Skin	Opera Film Produzione
1981	The Seduction	The Romantic Venture
1980	The Big Brawl	Warner Bros.
1980	Brubaker	Fox
1980	*The Competition	Columbia Pictures
1980	The Nude Bomb/The Return of Maxwell Smart	Universal
1980	The Serial	Columbia Pictures
1980	When Time Ran Out/Earth's Final Fury	Warner Bros.
1979	*The Amityville Horror	American International Pics.
1979	Boulevard Nights	Warner Bros.
1979	The Concorde/Airport '79	Universal
1979	Escape to Athena	Lord Leu Grade Productions
1979	Love and Bullets	MGM
1978	The Cat from Outer Space	Walt Disney Productions
1978	The Manitou	Manitou Productions Ltd.
1978	Nunzio	Universal

1977	The Day of the Animals	Film Ventures International
1977	The Eagle Has Landed	Associated General Films
1977	Rollercoaster	Universal
1977	Telefon	MGM
1976	Return from Witch Mountain	Walt Disney Productions
1976	The Sky Riders	Fox
1976	Special Delivery	Bing Crosby Productions
1976	St. Ives	Warner Bros.
1976	*Voyage of the Damned	Associated General Films
1975	The Four Musketeers/Milady's Revenge	Este Films
1975	The Master Gunfighter	Warner Bros.
1974	Golden Needles	Warner Bros.
1974	Man on a Swing	Paramount
1973	Charlie Varrick	Universal
1973	Enter the Dragon	Warner Bros.
1973	Harry in Your Pocket	United Artists
1973	Hit!	Paramount
1973	Magnum Force	Warner Bros.
1973	The Neptune Factor	Fox
1972	Joe Kidd	Universal
1972	Prime Cuts	Cinema Center Films
1972	Rage	Warner Bros.
1972	The Wrath of God	MGM
1971	The Beguiled	Universal
1971	The Christian Licorice Store	Cinema Center Films
1971	Dirty Harry	Warner Bros.
1971	The Hellstrom Chronicle	David Wolper Productions
1971	Mrs. Pollifax—Spy	Walt Disney Productions
1971	Pretty Maids All in a Row	MGM
1971	THX 1138	Zoetrope Productions
1970	I Love My Wife	David Wolper Productions
1970	Imago	Emerson Film Enterprises
1970	Kelly's Heroes	MGM
1970	Pussycat, Pussycat, I Love You	United Artists
1970	W.U.S.A.	Paramount
1969	Che!	Fox
1969	The Eye of the Cat	Universal
1968	The Brotherhood/The Heroin Gang	Paramount
1968	Bullitt	Warner Bros.

1968	Coogan's Bluff	Universal
1968	*The Fox	Warner Bros.
1968	Hell in the Pacific	American Broadcasting Co.
1968	Sol Madrid	MGM
1967	*Cool Hand Luke	Warner Bros.
1967	Murderers' Row	Columbia Pictures
1967	The President's Analyst	Paramount Pictures
1967	Sullivan's Empire	MGM
1967	The Venetian Affair	MGM
1967	Who's Minding the Mint?	Columbia Pictures
1966	Blindfold	Universal
1966	I Deal in Danger	20th Century Fox
	Television	
1966	The Liquidator	MGM
1966	Way . . . Way Out!	Fox
1965	The Cincinnati Kid	MGM
1965	Dark Intruder	Universal
1965	Gone with the Wave	Columbia Pictures– Screen Gems
1965	Once a Thief	MGM
1964	Joy House/Les Félins	MGM
1964	Rhino!	MGM
1957	El Jefe	Aries

* Academy Award Nomination

Television

1993	Danger Theatre	Fox
1991	El Quixote (mini-series)	Piedra Prod.
1991	A Woman Named Jackie (mini-series)	NBC
1990	Face to Face (television movie)	CBS
1989	Original Sin (television movie)	New World
1989	Neon Empire (television movie)	Fries Ent.
1988	Berlin Blues (television movie)	Canon Prod.
1988	Earth Star Voyager	Disney TV
1988	Shakedown on the Sunset Strip (television movie)	CBS
1987	Out on a Limb (mini-series)	ABC
1986	Beverly Hills Madam (television movie)	Orion Television

1985	A.D. (mini-series)	Int'l Film Corp.
1985	Command 5	Paramount
1985	The Equalizer (pilot)	Universal
1985	Hollywood Wives (mini-series)	Aaron Spelling
1985	Private Sessions (television movie)	CBS
1984	Glitter (television movie)	Aaron Spelling
1984	Little White Lies (television movie)	BBC
1984	Spraggue	Lorimar
1983	Princess Daisy (mini-series)	NBC
1983	Starflight One	Orlini Nelson
1982	Victims	Warner TV
1981	Chicago Story (television movie)	MGM Television
1981	Pay the Piper (television movie)	Paramount
1979	Quest (television movie)	MGM
1978	House Detective	Lorimar
1978	The Nativity (television movie)	20th Century Fox
1978	The President's Mistress (television movie)	Paramount
1977	Good Against Evil	20th Century Fox
1976	Brenda Starr (television movie)	Wolper
1975	Bronk (theme and episode)	MGM
1975	Delancey Street (television movie)	Paramount
1975	Foster and Laurie (television movie)	Chuck Fries Prod.
1975	Guilty or Innocent: The Sam Sheppard Murder Case (television movie)	Universal
1975	Starsky and Hutch (theme and episodes)	20th Century Fox
1974	Petrocelli (theme and episodes)	Paramount
1974	Planet of the Apes (theme and episodes)	20th Century Fox
1973	Egan (pilot)	Paramount
1973	Hunter (television movie)	CBS
1972	Private Eye	Universal TV
1972	Sixth Sense (television movie)	Universal
1972	Welcome Home, Johnny Bristol (television movie)	CBS
1971	I.F.M. (television movie)	20th Century Fox
1971	Memo from Purgatory (Alfred Hitchcock)	Universal

1971	The Partners	Universal
1971	The Virginians (episodes)	Universal
1970	The Aquarians (television movie)	Ivn Thor
1969	Medical Center (theme and episodes)	MGM
1969	The Young Lawyers (theme and episode)	Paramount
1968	Braddock (theme and segments)	20th Century Fox
1968	The Rise and Fall of the Third Reich	Wolper
1968	Wagon Train (episodes)	Universal
1967	How I Spent My Summer Vacation (television movie)	Universal
1967	Mannix (theme and episodes)	Paramount
1967	Shipwreck (television movie)	Universal
1967	Sullivan Country (television movie)	Universal
1967	Three for Danger (television movie)	Four Star
1966	The Doomsday Flight (television movie)	Universal
1966	The Hidden World of Insects	Wolper/Nat'l Geo.
1966	Jericho (television movie)	MGM
1966	Mission: Impossible (theme and episodes)	Paramount
1966	T.H.E. Cat (theme and episodes)	NBC
1966	The World of Jacques Yves Cousteau	Wolper
1965	Maryk (television movie)	Screen Gems
1965	The Way Out Men (television documentary)	Wolper
1964	The Black Cloak (television movie)	Universal
1964	The Blue Light (theme and episodes)	NBC/20th Century Fox
1964	The Highest Fall of All	Universal
1963	Kraft Suspense Theatre (episodes)	Universal
1963	90 Bristol Court (theme and episode)	Universal
1962	The Cliff Dwellers (television movie)	Bing Crosby Prod.
1961	Ben Casey (episode)	Screen Gems
1961	Dr. Kildare (theme and episodes)	MGM

Classical

2007	Elegy to Joseph Haydn	Commissioned by Austria in order to commemorate the

		second bicentennial of Joseph Haydn's death
2006	Concerto for Piano, Jazz Trumpet and Orchestra	Commissioned by the SMILE Foundation in Australia; premiered August 2007 at the Sydney Opera House with the Sydney Symphony
2004	Triple Concerto for Clarinet, Viola, Piano and Orchestra	Commissioned by the Halcyon Trio; premiered September 2004 with the New Jersey Symphony Orchestra
2003	Fantasy for Screenplay and Orchestra	Commissioned by the Chicago Symphony Orchestra; premiered October 2003
2001	Symphonic Impressions of Oman	Commissioned by the Omani government; recorded by the London Symphony Orchestra
2000	Jazz and Blues Variations, a Symphonic Celebration	Performed by the St. Louis Symphony Orchestra; commissioned by the AMTA (American Music Therapy Association), November 16, 2000; St. Louis, MO
1998	Divertimento pour les Ensemble des Violoncelles	Performed by the International Cello Festival in Beauvais, France
1997	Tango del Atardecer	Main theme from the film *Tango*, symphonic version
1996	Concierto Caribeno	Performed by Benjamin Juarez, Juan Carlos Laguna (guitar), Marisa Canales (flute); composed and conducted

		by Lalo Schifrin with the London Symphony Orchestra
1994	Homage a Ravel	Commissioned by the Eaken Piano Trio, Dickinson College
1993	Symphony No. 1 (Queen Lili'Uokalani)	Commissioned by Lili'Uokalani Foundation in memoriam of the last queen of Hawaii; performed by the Honolulu Symphony Orchestra; recorded by the Vienna Symphony Orchestra
1992	Cantares Argentinos	Commissioned by the Los Angeles Master Chorale
1991	Piano Concerto No. 2 (The Americas)	Commissioned by the Steinway Foundation
1990	Impresiones Fantasy for Trumpet and Orchestra	Commissioned by Doc Severinsen; performed by the Glendale Symphony Orchestra, October 1990
1989	The Trial of Louis XVI (opera)	Commissioned by Placido Domingo
1988	Cantos Aztecas (Cantata)	Commissioned by the Mexico City Philharmonic Orchestra; premiered October 1988 by Placido Domingo, the Mexico City Philharmonic Orchestra, and the Archeological Museum of Mexico; based on ancient Aztec poetry by the twelfth-century prince Nexahualcoyotl

1988	Dances Concertantes for Clarinet and Orchestra	Commissioned by the Kansas City Symphony Orchestra
1987	La Nouvelle Orleans for Woodwind Quintet	Commissioned and recorded by the Dorian Woodwind Quintet
1987	Pan American Games Overture	Commissioned by Disneyworld and CBS
1987	Resonances for Piano	Commissioned by Paulina Drake
1986	Concerto for Double Bass Orchestra	Commissioned by Gary Karr; recorded by the Paris Philharmonic Orchestra
1986	Romerias: Guitar Solo	Commissioned by Angel Romero
1986	Statue of Liberty (A Symphonic Celebration)	Premiered July 4, 1968, at the Hollywood Bowl with the Glendale Symphony Orchestra
1986	Three Tangos for Flute, Harp and Strings	Commissioned by the Los Angeles Chamber Orchestra
1985	Piano Concerto #1	Commissioned by the Mexico City Philharmonic Orchestra
1984	Central Park Variations for Clarinet and Piano	Commissioned by David Shifrin
1984	Concerto for Guitar and Orchestra	Recorded by Angel Romero and the London Philharmonic Orchestra
1983	Tropicos	Premiered by the American Chamber Orchestra
1980	Capriccio for Clarinet and Strings	Commissioned by the Israel Philharmonic Orchestra
1980	Invocations for Orchestra	Commissioned by the New American Orchestra
1973	Journeys (for One Percussionist Playing 100 Instruments)	Commissioned by the University of Southern California

1973	Movement for Strings	
1972	Madrigals for the Space Age Text by Ray Bradbury	Commissioned by the Roger Wagner Chorale
1970	Dialogues for Jazz Quintet and Orchestra	Commissioned by Cannonball Adderley; recorded for Capitol Records
1970	Pulsations for Symphony Orchestra, Jazz Band and Electronic Instruments	Commissioned by the Los Angeles Philharmonic Orchestra
1969	Continuum for Harp	Commissioned by the American Harp Association
1967	Cantata for the Rise and Fall of the Third Reich	Commissioned by the Los Angeles Philharmonic Orchestra
1967	Symphonic Sketches of Cool Hand Luke	
1966	The Jazz Mass	Commissioned by RCA and the Vatican
1966	Cantata: You Shall Not Make War Anymore	Commissioned by the University of Judaism
1966	Gesualdo Variants for 16 Instruments	Commissioned by the Ojai Music Festival
1965	Canons for String Quartet	Commissioned by the Los Angeles String Quartet
1964	Innovations	Commissioned by Stan Kenton and the Neophonic Orchestra
1963	Labyrinth	Commissioned by the Canadian Broadcasting Corporation
1963	Study in Rhythm	Commissioned by the Canadian Broadcasting Corporation
1963	Variations for Percussion, Strings, Harp and Cellesta	Commissioned by the Los Angeles Philharmonic Orchestra

1962	Jazz Faust (ballet)	Commissioned by President Kennedy's Commission of the Arts
1962	The Ritual of Sound	Commissioned by Gunther Schuller and the Carnegie Hall Chamber Orchestra
1961	New Continent Suite for Trumpet, Wind and Percussion	Commissioned by the Monterey Jazz Festival
1960	Gillespiana Suite for Trumpet and Brass	Commissioned by Dizzy Gillespie

Discography

The Enforcer
Lalo Schifrin
Composer/Conductor
Aleph Records/2007

Abominable
Lalo Schifrin
Composer/Conductor
Aleph Records/2006

Letters from Argentina
Lalo Schifrin
Composer/Conductor
Aleph Records/2006

Shifrin Plays Schifrin
Lalo Schifrin
Composer/Conductor
Aleph Records/2006

Caveman
Lalo Schifrin
Composer/Conductor
Aleph Records/2005

Les Félins
Lalo Schifrin
Composer/Conductor
Aleph Records/2005

**Kaleidoscope: Jazz Meets the
  Symphony #6**
Lalo Schifrin
Composer/Conductor
Aleph Records/2005

Magnum Force
Lalo Schifrin
Composer/Conductor
Aleph Records/2005

Dirty Harry
Lalo Schifrin
Composer/Conductor
Aleph Records/2004

The Hellstrom Chronicle
Lalo Schifrin
Composer/Conductor
Aleph Records/2004

**Ins and Outs/Lalo Live at the Blue
  Note**
Lalo Schifrin
Composer/Conductor
Aleph Records/2003

Symphonic Impressions of Oman
London Symphony Orchestra
Lalo Schifrin
Composer/Conductor
Scherzo Music/2003

The Amityville Horror
Lalo Schifrin
Composer/Conductor
Aleph Records/2002

The Cincinnati Kid
Lalo Schifrin
Composer/Conductor
Aleph Records/2002

Return of the Marquis De Sade
Lalo Schifrin
Composer/Conductor
Aleph Records/2002

Cool Hand Luke
Lalo Schifrin
Composer/Conductor
Aleph Records/2001

**Intersections: Jazz Meets the
  Symphony #5**
Lalo Schifrin
Composer/Conductor
Aleph Records/2001

Rollercoaster
Lalo Schifrin
Composer/Conductor
Aleph Records/2001

**Schifrin Conducts Stravinsky,
  Schifrin and Ravel**
Lalo Schifrin
Composer/Conductor
Aleph Records/2001

Brazilian Jazz
Lalo Schifrin
Performer
Aleph Records/2000

Esperanto
Lalo Schifrin
Composer/Conductor
Aleph Records/2000

The Fox
Lalo Schifrin
Composer/Conductor
Aleph Records/2000

Jazz Goes to Hollywood
Lalo Schifrin
Composer/Conductor
Aleph Records/2000

Cantos Aztecas
Lalo Schifrin
Composer/Conductor
Aleph Records/1999

The Eagle Has Landed
Lalo Schifrin
Composer/Conductor
Aleph Records/1999

Jazz Meets the Symphony #5
  (boxed set)
Lalo Schifrin
Composer/Conductor
Aleph Records/1999

Latin Jazz Suite
Lalo Schifrin
Composer/Conductor
Aleph Records/1999

Mannix
Lalo Schifrin
Composer/Conductor
Aleph Records/1999

The Osterman Weekend
Lalo Schifrin
Composer/Conductor
Aleph Records/1999

Something to Believe In
(soundtrack)
Lalo Schifrin
Composer/Conductor
Aleph Records/1999

Arias . . . Cesar Hernandez
Cesar Hernandez
Lalo Schifrin
Arranger/Conductor
Aleph Records/1998
Also available on: Urtext Digital
     Classics

Che!
Lalo Schifrin
Composer/Arranger/Conductor/
     Piano/Producer
Aleph Records/1998

Dirty Harry Anthology
Lalo Schifrin
Composer
Aleph Records/1998

Film Classics
Lalo Schifrin presents 100 years of

cinema with Julia Migenes and
     Dee Dee Bridgewater
Lalo Schifrin
Arranger/Conductor/Piano/
     Producer
Aleph Records/1998

Gillespiana
New recording of the classic with
     the WDR Big Band in Cologne,
     Germany
Lalo Schifrin
Composer/Arranger/Conductor/
     Piano/Producer
Aleph Records/1998

Jazz Suite on the Mass Texts
Lalo Schifrin
Composer/Conductor
Aleph Records/1998

Lili'Uokalani Symphony
Lalo Schifrin
Composer/Conductor
Urtext Digital Classics/1998

**Metamorphosis: Jazz Meets the
     Symphony #4**
Lalo Schifrin
Composer/Arranger/Conductor/
     Producer
Aleph Records/1998

Rush Hour (film score)
Lalo Schifrin
Composer/Conductor
Aleph Records/1998

Christmas in Vienna
Jose Carreras, Placido Domingo,
     Diana Ross
Lalo Schifrin

Arranger
Sony/1997

**Concierto Caribeno for Flute and
  Orchestra**
Lalo Schifrin/Marisa Canales/Juan
  Carlos Laguna
Lalo Schifrin
Composer/Conductor
Auvidis Travelling/1997

A Celebration of Christmas
Jose Carreras, Natalie Cole, Placido
  Domingo
Lalo Schifrin
Arranger
Erato/Elektra/1996

**Those Fabulous Hollywood
  Marches**
San Diego Symphony
Lalo Schifrin
Conductor
Pro-Arte/1996

**Firebird: Jazz Meets the Symphony
  #3**
Lalo Schifrin
Composer/Arranger/Piano/
  Conductor/Producer
East West/Four Winds/1995

**Carreras, Domingo and Pavarotti
  in Concert**
Jose Carreras, Placido Domingo,
  Luciano Pavarotti
Lalo Schifrin
Arranger
London/1994

Julia Migenes in Vienna
Julia Migenes

Lalo Schifrin
Conductor
Erato/1994

More Jazz Meets the Symphony
Lalo Schifrin
Composer/Arranger/Piano/
  Conductor/Producer
Atlantic/1994

The Three Tenors in Concert 1994
Placido Domingo, Luciano
  Pavarotti, Jose Carreras, Zubin
  Mehta
Lalo Schifrin
Arranger
Atlantic/1994

Cantos Aztecas
Placido Domingo
Lalo Schifrin
Composer/Conductor
Pro-Arte/1993

Jazz Meets the Symphony
Lalo Schifrin
Composer/Arranger/Producer
Atlantic/1993

Swinging Baroque Te Deum
Maurice Andre
Lalo Schifrin
Arranger/Conductor
Erato/1993

Amigos Para Siempre
Jose Carreras
Lalo Schifrin
Arranger/Conductor/Producer
Warners/1992

Carnival of the Animals
Various

Lalo Schifrin
Conductor
Dove Audio/1992

Romancing the Film
Lalo Schifrin
Conductor
Pro-Arte/1992

Don Quixote
Lalo Schifrin
Composer/Conductor
Prometheus/1991

**Astor Piazzolla: Concierto Para
   Bandoneon/Tres Tangos**
Astor Piazzolla
Lalo Schifrin
Conductor
Elektra/1990

Dorian Wind Quintet
Dorian Wind Quintet
Lalo Schifrin
Composer
Summit/1990

Hitchcock: Master of Mayhem
San Diego Symphony
Lalo Schifrin
Conductor
Pro-Arte/1990

Berlin Blues
Julia Migenes
Lalo Schifrin
Composer/Arranger
Milan/1988

Weekend in L.A.
George Benson
Composer
Warner Bros./1988

Fourth Protocol
Lalo Schifrin
Soundtrack
Film Trax/1987

Telly Hits 2
Lalo Schifrin
Composer
BBC Stylus/1986

Anno Domini
Lalo Schifrin
Conductor
Prometheus/1985

Let It Live
Sarah Vaughan
Lalo Schifrin
Soundtrack
Rive Records/1985

Guitar Concerto
Angel Romero
London Philharmonic
Lalo Schifrin
Composer
EMI/1984

The Osterman Weekend
Lalo Schifrin
Soundtrack
Varese Sarabande/1983

Sudden Impact
Lalo Schifrin
Soundtrack
Viva/1983

Ins and Outs
Lalo Schifrin
Composer/Arranger/Piano Solo
Palo Alto Records/1982

The Sting II
Lalo Schifrin
Soundtrack
MCA/1982

La Peau
Lalo Schifrin
Soundtrack
Gaumont Musique/1981

La Pelle
Lalo Schifrin
Soundtrack
Cinevox/1981

Battle Creek Brawl
Lalo Schifrin
Soundtrack
Victor/1980

The Cat Strikes Again
Jimmy Smith (Composer)
Lalo Schifrin
Conductor/Arranger
Wersi/1980

The Competition
Lalo Schifrin
Soundtrack/Conductor/
  Composer
MCA/1980

The Amityville Horror
Lalo Schifrin
Soundtrack
Casablanca/1979

Boulevard Nights
Lalo Schifrin
Soundtrack
Warner Bros./1979

Children of the World
Stan Getz

Lalo Schifrin
Producer/Composer/Conductor
Columbia/1979

Fire and Ice
Lalo Schifrin
Producer/Composer
MCA/1979

**New Horizons for Jazz Ensemble
  Vol. 3**
Lalo Schifrin
Piano Solo
Jenson/1979

No One Home
Lalo Schifrin
Producer/Composer/Arranger
Tabu/1979

Wet
Barbra Streisand
Lalo Schifrin
Composer/Arranger/Conductor
CBS/1979

Dream Machine
Paul Horn (Producer)
Lalo Schifrin
Composer/Conductor
Mushroom Records/1978

Great Adventure Film Scores
Lalo Schifrin
Composer/Conductor
Entr'acte/1978

Gypsies
Lalo Schifrin
Producer/Composer/Keyboards
Tabu/1978

Nunzio
Lalo Schifrin

Soundtrack
MCA/1978

Rain Dance
Anthony Ortega
Lalo Schifrin
Composer
Discovery Records/1978

Free Ride
Dizzy Gillespie (Producer)
Lalo Schifrin
Composer/Arranger
Pablo/1977

Harp Aujourd'hui
Marcella Decray
Lalo Schifrin
Composer
Coronet/1977

Rollercoaster
Lalo Schifrin
Soundtrack
MCA/1977

Voyage of the Damned
Lalo Schifrin
Soundtrack
Entr'acte/1977

Black Widow
Lalo Schifrin
Jazz Artist/Arranger/Synthesizer
  Solo
CTI/1976

Jaws
Lalo Schifrin
Arranger/Conductor/Keyboards
CTI/1976

Towering Toccata
Lalo Schifrin

Keyboard Solo/Conductor/
  Arranger
CTI/1976

**Ann Mason Stockton Plays Music
  for the Harp**
Ann Mason Stockton
Lalo Schifrin
Composer
Crystal/1973

Enter the Dragon
Lalo Schifrin
Soundtrack
Warner Bros./1973

La Clave
Lalo Schifrin
Composer/Piano Solo
Verve/1972

Remus 5
Alfredo Remus
Lalo Schifrin
Composer
Disco Es Cuture/1972

Rock Requiem
Lalo Schifrin
Composer/Conductor/Producer
Verve/1971

Bullitt
Wilton Felder
Lalo Schifrin
Composer
World Pacific Jazz/1970

Kelly's Heroes
Lalo Schifrin
Soundtrack
MGM/1970

Lalo Schifrin in Buenos Aires
Lalo Schifrin

Piano Solo
RCA/1970

Medical Center and Other Great Themes
Lalo Schifrin
Soundtrack
MGM/1970

Tristeza on Piano
Oscar Peterson Trio
Lalo Schifrin
Composer
BASF/1970

Cannonball Adderley
Cannonball Adderley Quintet and Orchestra
Lalo Schifrin
Composer/Conductor
Capitol/1969

Che!
Lalo Schifrin
Soundtrack
Tetragrammaton/1969

Mannix
Lalo Schifrin
Soundtrack
Paramount/1969

Bullitt
Lalo Schifrin
Soundtrack
Warner Bros./1968

Down Here on the Ground
Wes Montgomery
Lalo Schifrin
Composer
A&M/1968

Down Here on the Ground
Gogi Grant

Lalo Schifrin
Composer
Pete Records/1968

The Fox
Lalo Schifrin
Soundtrack
Warner Bros./1968

More Mission: Impossible
Lalo Schifrin
Soundtrack
Paramount/1968

The Other Side of Lalo Schifrin
Lalo Schifrin
Piano Solo
Audio Fidelity/1968

There's a Whole Lalo Schifrin Going On
Lalo Schifrin
Composer/Conductor
Dot/1968

Cool Hand Luke
Lalo Schifrin
Soundtrack
Dot/1967

Mission: Impossible
Lalo Schifrin
Soundtrack
MCA/1967
Grammy Award winner: Best Instrumental Theme
Grammy Award winner: Best Original Score Written for a Motion Picture or Television Show

The Rise and Fall of the Third Reich
Lalo Schifrin

Soundtrack
MGM/1967

Marquis De Sade
Lalo Schifrin
Composer/Arranger/Keyboards/
   Conductor
Verve/1966

The Cincinnati Kid
Lalo Schifrin
Soundtrack
MGM/1965

The Liquidator
Lalo Schifrin
Soundtrack
MGM/1965

Once a Thief
Lalo Schifrin
Soundtrack
Verve/1965

Sol Madrid
Lalo Schifrin
Soundtrack
MGM/1965

The Cat
Jimmy Smith (Composer)
Lalo Schifrin
Conductor/Arranger
Verve/1964
Grammy Award winner: Best
   Original Jazz Composition

Explorations
Louie Bellson
Lalo Schifrin
Composer/Conductor
Roulette/1964

Gone with the Wave
Lalo Schifrin

Composer/Arranger
Colpix Records/1964

In the Name of Love
Peggy Lee
Lalo Schifrin
Composer/Arranger
Capitol/1964

Jazz Suite on the Mass Texts
Paul Horn
Lalo Schifrin
Composer/Conductor
RCA/1964
Grammy Award winner: Best
   Original Jazz Composition

New Fantasy
Dizzy Gillespie
Lalo Schifrin
Composer/Piano Solo
Verve/1964

Sweet 'n Sassy
Sarah Vaughan
Lalo Schifrin
Conductor/Arranger
Roulette/1964

**Between Broadway and
   Hollywood**
Lalo Schifrin
Piano Solo
MGM/1963

Bossa Nova
Quincy Jones
Lalo Schifrin
Piano Solo
Mercury/1963

Bossa Nova
Luiz Bonfa
Lalo Schifrin

Conductor/Arranger
Verve/1963

Bossa Nova
Eddie Harris
Lalo Schifrin
Piano Solo/Arranger
Vee-Jay/1963

Eso Es Latin Jazz . . . Man
Antonio Diaz Mena Piano Solo
Lalo Schifrin
Arranger
Audio Fidelity/1963

Johnny Hodges
Johnny Hodges
Lalo Schifrin
Composer/Piano Solo
Verve/1963

Several Shades of Jade
Cal Tjader
Lalo Schifrin
Composer/Arranger/Conductor
Verve/1963

Yellow Canary
Lalo Schifrin
Piano Solo
Verve/1963

Bossa Nova: New Brazilian Jazz
Lalo Schifrin
Conductor/Arranger/Piano Solo
Audio Fidelity/1962

Desafinado
Pat Thomas
Lalo Schifrin
Conductor/Arranger
MGM/1962

Dizzy Gillespie at Carnegie Hall
Dizzy Gillespie (Composer)
Lalo Schifrin
Arranger/Piano Solo
Verve/1962

Dizzy on the French Riviera
Dizzy Gillespie (Composer)
Lalo Schifrin
Arranger/Piano Solo
Philips/1962

Insensatez
Lalo Schifrin with Strings
Piano Solo/Conductor
Verve/1962

Piano, Strings and Bossa Nova
Lalo Schifrin
Piano Solo/Conductor/Arranger
MGM/1962

**Dizzy Gillespie Rarities
  1944–1961**
Dizzy Gillespie
Lalo Schifrin
Piano Solo
Raretone/1961

An Electrifying Evening
Dizzy Gillespie
Lalo Schifrin
Piano Solo
Verve/1961

Jazz at the Philharmonic
Lalo Schifrin
Piano Solo
Verve/1961

A Musical Safari
Dizzy Gillespie (Arranger)

Lalo Schifrin
Composer/Piano Solo
Booman/1961

Gillespiana
Dizzy Gillespie
Lalo Schifrin
Composer/Conductor
Verve/1960

Lalole
Lalo Schifrin Piano Solo with Strings
Arranger/Conductor
Roulette/1958

Spectrum
Lalo Schifrin
Composer/Arranger
Epic/1957

Index

~

About the Author

Lalo Schifrin is a true Renaissance man. As a pianist, composer, and conductor, he is equally at home conducting a symphony orchestra, performing at an international jazz festival, scoring a film or television show, or creating works for the Los Angeles Chamber Orchestra, the London Philharmonic, and even the Sultan of Oman.

Lalo Schifrin received classical training in music at the Paris Conservatory during the early 1950s and simultaneously became a professional jazz pianist, composer, and arranger, playing and recording in Europe. After hearing Schifrin play with his own big concert band in Buenos Aires, Dizzy Gillespie asked him to become his pianist and arranger. In 1958, Schifrin moved to the United States and thus began a remarkable career.

Schifrin has written more than sixty classical compositions and more than one hundred scores for films and television, including *Mission: Impossible*, *Mannix*, *Cool Hand Luke*, *Bullitt*, *Dirty Harry*, *The Amityville Horror*, and the *Rush Hour* films. To date, Schifrin has won four Grammy Awards (with twenty-one nominations), won one Cable ACE Award, and received six Oscar nominations.

Schifrin was appointed musical director of the Paris Philharmonic Orchestra in 1987, a position he held for two years. Among Schifrin's other conducting credits are the London Philharmonic Orchestra, the London Symphony Orchestra, the Vienna Symphony Orchestra, the Los Angeles Philharmonic, the Israel Philharmonic, the Houston Symphony Orchestra, the Los Angeles Chamber Orchestra, the Mexico City Philharmonic, the

Orchestra of Saint Luke (New York City), and the National Symphony Orchestra of Argentina.

He was commissioned to write the grand finale to celebrate the finals of the World Cup soccer championship in Caracalla, Italy, in July 1990. In this concert, the Three Tenors, Luciano Pavarotti, Placido Domingo, and Jose Carreras, sang together for the first time. Schifrin also arranged the sequels for the Three Tenors at the subsequent World Cup finals, in July 1994 at Dodger Stadium; July 1998 in Paris, France; and June 2002 in Japan.

Schifrin's most recent commissions include *Fantasy for Screenplay and Orchestra*, for Daniel Barenboim and the Chicago Symphony, and *Symphonic Impressions of Oman*, commissioned by the Sultan of Oman, recorded in England with the London Symphony Orchestra and released by Schifrin's own record label, Aleph Records, in 2003.

It is Schifrin's ability to switch musical gears that makes him so unique in the music world. As a jazz musician he has performed and recorded with great personalities such as Dizzy Gillespie, Sarah Vaughan, Ella Fitzgerald, Stan Getz, and Count Basie. His longtime involvement in both the jazz and symphonic worlds came together in 1993 when he was featured as pianist and conductor for his on-going series of *Jazz Meets the Symphony* recordings, with the London Philharmonic Orchestra and such notable jazz stars as Ray Brown, Grady Tate, Jon Faddis, Paquito D'Rivera, and James Morrison. The third of the series, *Firebird: Jazz Meets the Symphony #3* (1996), received two Grammy nominations. Aleph Records released *Kaleidoscope: Jazz Meets the Symphony #6* in August 2005, recorded at the Sydney Opera House in Australia. Schifrin was invited back to Australia in 2006 to conduct a Jazz Meets the Symphony tour in Queensland, Adelaide, and Sydney. In 2006, Schifrin returned to Australia for the world premiere of his Double Concerto for Piano, Trumpet, and Orchestra, commissioned by the SMILE Foundation.

In April 2005, Schifrin premiered *Letters from Argentina*, a piece combining tango and Argentinean folk music with classical music to create a fresh new sound reminiscent of his homeland. It premiered at Lincoln Center with Schifrin on piano, David Shifrin on clarinet, Cho-Liang "Jimmy" Lin on violin, Nestor Marconi on bandoneon, Pablo Aslan on contrabass, and Satoshi Takeishi on percussion. These distinguished soloists toured the United States that summer, performing in Portland, Oregon; Santa Fe, New Mexico; and La Jolla, California. The piece was recorded and released on Aleph Records in May 2006.

Lalo Schifrin is a recipient of the 1988 BMI Lifetime Achievement Award. BMI also honored Schifrin in 2001 with a special composer's award for his original cult classic theme to *Mission: Impossible*. He was most recently honored for his significant contribution to music, film, and culture by the French performing rights organization SACEM, along with the 57th Annual Cannes Film Festival in 2004. That same year he was awarded the 65th Annual Golden Score Award by the American Society of Music Arrangers and Composers (ASMAC). He has been honored by the City of Los Angeles, the Los Angeles County, and the California Legislature, and he received a star on the Hollywood Walk of Fame in 1988. He also received the Distinguished Artist Award in 1998 from the Los Angeles Music Center, and he recently established a jazz and classical composition scholarship in his name for UCLA. He was honored by the Israeli government for his "Contributions to World Understanding through Music," and he was given honorary doctorate degrees from the Rhode Island School of Design and the University of La Plata, Argentina. Lalo Schifrin has been appointed Chevalier de l'Ordre des Arts et Lettres, one of the highest distinctions granted by France's Minister of Culture, and in 1998, the Argentine government appointed him Advisor to the President in Cultural Affairs with a rank of Secretary of the Cabinet.

Schifrin has been married to his wife, Donna, for more than thirty years. His three children include William, a writer for films and television; Frances, an art director/designer; and Ryan, a film writer/director. Schifrin scored Ryan's first horror feature film, *Abominable*, which was released in 2006. For more information on Lalo Schifrin, please visit www.schifrin.com.

~

About the Editor

Dr. Richard Palmer is director of general education at Bedford School, UK, where for twenty years he was head of English. He was educated at Dulwich College, Cambridge University, and the University of East Anglia, where his doctoral thesis examined the work of Norman Mailer. A staff writer for *Jazz Journal International* for thirty years, he has written widely on jazz, educational, and literary subjects, and he has published fifteen books thus far; the more recent include *Sonny Rollins* and *Philip Larkin's Jazz Writings*. He was editor/consultant for Oscar Peterson's 2001 autobiography *My Life in Jazz*, and he publishes regularly in educational and literary journals. He is the author of *Such Deliberate Disguises: The Art of Philip Larkin* (2008).